PRAISE FOR *ME*

"Both my military and pilot experiences taught me the importance [?] disciplined thinking and leadership decision-making. Dave's book, *Mega Thinking*, provides a simple, powerful way to achieve this. I highly recommend that you read it."

> **John Kerr**—TOPGUN graduate/instructor, US Navy
> Rear Admiral (retired), Delta Airlines captain (retired),
> and currently captain on a private B767 and B737

"The Computer History Museum addresses important topics such as the internet, entrepreneurship, and AI. As a long-term member of our Board of Trustees, Dave and I have worked closely together. I admire his structured way of thinking about strategic issues and leadership decision-making. In *Mega Thinking*, Dave lays out a surprisingly easy process to develop a well-structured set of thoughts relating to any complex leadership decision. Anyone facing decisions about complicated topics will benefit from reading this book."

> **Steve Smith**—Chair, Board of Trustees at Computer
> History Museum and retired technology executive

"Dave Martin shows us the way to think better and more successfully in *Mega Thinking*. Building on the shoulders of giants in thinking and philosophy—along with practical, real-life examples—Dave presents a step-by-step process to improve your thinking and, therefore, be a better leader. Thank you, Dave, for this important work and contribution to our world."

> **Ray Rothrock**—Nuclear Engineer, Venture Capitalist, Cyber
> Security and Nuclear Expert, University Trustee and Author

"During the thirty years I have known Dave Martin, I have successfully coached NFL and collegiate football teams, while Dave has been a successful CEO and has coached many other CEOs. Both require smart thinking and excellent decision-making. I tease Dave that as a football coach I have to make decisions in a second, and as CEO he has weeks or an entire season!

Even so, leadership decisions must be well thought out. Every coach and leader should read *Mega Thinking* to apply its simple, powerful approach to better thinking."

Mike Shanahan— Superbowl-Winning NFL Coach and Division 1 and 2 Collegiate Championship Coach

"I admire how Dave Martin, a fellow author and coach of leaders, has crafted *Mega Thinking*. This book provides a highly practical process for thinking smarter and making even better leadership decisions. It is a must-read for anyone looking to level up these skills and positively impact their lives. I will be recommending it to my own clients."

Chris Janssen, MA, BCC—Results Coach and bestselling author of *Living All In: How to Show Up for the Life You Want*

"I have known Dave for over thirty years, as we have served on boards of directors together and helped form the Computer History Museum Exponential Center, which is focused on inspiring entrepreneurship. Dave's book is provoking in its pragmatic suggestions to improve everyday thinking. This book provides a practical roadmap for more efficient thought and improved decision-making."

Larry Sonsini—Founder and Senior Partner of Wilson Sonsini, the leading law firm serving the technology industry

"From a wealth of real-world experience and a profound understanding of effective leadership, Dave Martin crafted a compelling, practical guide that inspires. This book is a must-read for anyone who aspires to lead with vision and integrity in the fast-paced and ever-changing business landscape of today. His insights are profound, actionable, and an indispensable resource for leaders at all levels."

Dr. Martin Eichelberger—Pediatric Surgeon, Founder of Safe Kids Worldwide, Founder and CEO of Triaj and Chairman of the WHIS Advisory Board on Digital Health and Pediatrics

MEGA
THINKING

A Simple, Powerful Process to
Think Smarter and Make
Better Leadership
Decisions

DAVE MARTIN

Mega Thinking: A Simple, Powerful Process to Think Smarter and Make Better Leadership Decisions
Published by The Tiger Media

Saratoga, California

ISBN: 979-8-9907684-0-6
BUSINESS & ECONOMICS / Leadership

Book research by Brennan McDonald

Cover design by Victoria Wolf, wolfdesignandmarketing.com. Copyright owned by Dave Martin.

Editing by Patrice Rhoades-Baum

THE
TIGER
MEDIA

BOOK SUMMARY

T he more you get out of *Mega Thinking* the more you will think smarter, make better leadership decisions, and be more fulfilled and successful. The MegaCepts—the greatest thoughts—regarding how to get the most out of this book are:

- Take the initial readership quiz that asks you how important thinking is in your life. Then commit yourself to focusing on how to think more and think smarter.

- Actively think about what you are reading in every chapter and what the greatest thoughts are in every chapter.

- Write those greatest thoughts down at the end of each chapter.

- Before reading Chapters 5 through 10, which apply the MegaCepts process to six different topics, think about what your initial ideas are about each topic.

- At the end of this book, write down your ideas on the thesis and MegaCepts of this book. Then compare them to the author's thesis and MegaCepts to arrive at your final list. Then post that list in multiple places to continuously remind yourself about this book's greatest thoughts on thinking.

- Talk to others whom you respect and believe would be interested in thinking smarter and pursuing better leadership decision-making. The more you talk about it, the more you will think about it. And the more you think about it, the more you will understand this simple, powerful process—and all of that is good!

CONTENTS

.

CHAPTER 1

INTRODUCTION TO MEGA THINKING:
How Great Thinking Helps You Make Better Leadership Decisions

"Reading furnishes the mind only with materials of knowledge; it is thinking that makes what we read ours."

—JOHN LOCKE

Thinking is perhaps the most powerful and important capability for every human being. It is even the reason why humans stay alive. Scientific research confirms that the brain's thinking occurs at two levels: subconscious and conscious. Subconscious thoughts include feelings, memories, and processes that occur below the level of conscious awareness. Conscious thinking applies to simple topics such as preparing a shopping list or getting dressed. More importantly, it applies to more complex topics, such as taking a test in school or being the leader of a company or institution.

Thinking about these more complex topics requires a structured and organized approach. That is what the thesis of this book is all about: *Mega Thinking, or great thinking, can be achieved by using a simple, powerful process to make better leadership decisions. This process enables you to define the ten or fewer MegaCepts, or greatest thoughts, on any topic. The ability to make better personal and professional leadership decisions leads to a better, more fulfilling, and successful life.*

So, to repeat for simplicity:

- Mega Thinking, or great thinking, is focused on thinking smarter about more complex topics.

- This book gives you a simple, powerful process for thinking smarter.

- The process is built on the principle of MegaCepts or greatest thoughts. Any topic can be best thought about by defining the ten or fewer greatest thoughts on that topic.

- Great thinking and the greatest thoughts result in smarter thinking, which in turn leads to making better leadership decisions in your personal and professional life.

- This leads to a better, more fulfilling, and successful life.

Some people ask, "How can a simple process be powerful?" I believe that once you have read this book you will agree the process is both simple and powerful. But, in the meantime, let's illustrate a few simple but powerful examples:

- **The Theory of Relativity:** This most powerful Albert Einstein theory is completely captured in the simple equation $E=mc^2$.

- **The Golden Rule:** This powerful, universal rule for how to treat people is simply, "Do unto others as you would have them do unto you."

- **The US Bill of Rights—Amendment I:** The simple but powerful right to freedom of religion, speech, assembly, and to petition the government for redress of grievances.

I wrote this book, because I wanted to share my fifty years of positive experience and success by applying the MegaCepts process. This resulted in making better leadership decisions for my personal and professional life and contributing to better decisions for my family and friends' personal lives. I have religiously applied the process in my professional life. I have also strategically advised and coached hundreds of other professionals and leaders who have experienced similar success by applying the process, thinking smarter, and making better leadership decisions.

By sharing the MegaCepts process with you and as many other people as possible, I hope and believe it will have a meaningful and positive impact on your lives. At this point you might be asking yourself, "Who is this author, what credentials does he have to write a book about thinking, and why should I listen to him and trust him about all of this?" My more detailed answer to these questions will be evident upon reading this book. The short answer is:

- This book is about explaining, illustrating, practicing, and understanding the details in support of the above thesis!

- To effectively write this book, I needed to have extensively and successfully used and educated others to use the MegaCepts process. This book is not based on academic theory; it is based on practical experience and success.

- This is exactly what I have done for myself and hundreds of other leaders. As I've applied and taught the MegaCepts process over the decades, I have earned referenceable credentials and a reputation with these leaders that include the formal and informal titles of Strategic Thinker and Planner, Close and Trusted Confidant, Experienced and Successful Leader, and Wise Coach.

After you have read this book, my goal is that you will have learned enough about me and my thinking experiences—as well as enough about Mega Thinking and its benefits for you—that you will simply close the book and think, "Thanks Coach." That would make all my effort to write and publish this book worthwhile.

Much more about the MegaCepts process will follow, but first let's provide more context for this most important topic of thinking smarter. Life is all about leadership and decision-making in your personal life, educational experience, and professional career. And thinking smarter leads to better leadership decisions, which in turn leads to a better and more successful life.

How I Discovered the MegaCepts Process

I discovered the MegaCepts process during my freshman year at Princeton University. My major was aeronautical engineering, in part because my high school guidance counselor Doris recommended it since I was good in math and science and because I could, "Help the United States beat the Russians in missiles and space." The Russians had launched and put in orbit the first space satellite, named *Sputnik I*, in 1957.

All engineering major students at Princeton were required to take Physics 101 as a prerequisite to entering engineering school. Physics 101 was a notoriously hard course, made even more intimidating, since it was taught in the same building where Albert Einstein did his world-changing research, including his Theory of Relativity.

Every Friday, the Physics 101 professor gave us a quiz. Every quiz presented four complex problems to solve, and each problem was worth ten points if you answered it correctly, or you could receive partial credit if you were "on the right track." The highest possible score was forty points, and the lowest was zero. Every Saturday morning, the professor posted the test results outside the lecture hall, with the highest scores at the top and the lowest scores at the bottom.

I'll never forget going to see the test results after the first week of my freshman year. I was on my way to football practice, and I stopped by the physics building to see my test result. I thought I did okay, so I searched for my name and score at the top of the list. There were about 150 students in the class, so it was a long list. When I got to the middle and still couldn't find my name, I started to get a little worried. I finally found my name near the bottom of the list and saw that my score was only five! I was devastated, especially since I had been a really good student in high school, getting As in all my classes, including math and science. There were some scores below mine, including several zeros, but that didn't make me feel any better.

I left feeling a bit scared and depressed but had to continue to the football stadium for a three-hour football practice. Fortunately, that took my mind off the quiz score. It is hard to think about test scores when you are running with the football and about to be tackled by a big, nasty linebacker. But the minute I finished practice and showered I started worrying again, so I went back to the physics building to check my score once more to make sure I had seen it correctly. Unfortunately, the score hadn't changed, it was still a five.

So, I decided to look back at the top of the list and saw that a few students had gotten the maximum forty points. One of them was Jim, whom I had just met and who lived in my freshman dorm. I decided to ask him how he was able to be so smart and get a perfect score. He was a nice guy and said he would be happy to share pointers about how he did so well.

Before we met, he asked me to bring my Physics 101 notebook in which I kept notes from the classes and lectures. When we sat down to work, he asked me to show him my notes from the prior week's lectures. I had filled over four pages with detailed notes. He then showed me his notes from the same lecture, and he had less than half a page. He told me that I was focused on what the professor was saying, not thinking about what the information meant. His notes captured what he thought were the key concepts that the professor was trying to communicate!

As I thought about what Jim was saying, I realized there is an even higher level of thought than just "key concepts." I thought about an aeronautical engineering project I was working on that involved a wind tunnel test. It was a complex project, and I had defined about twenty concepts that I was going to research. However, by focusing on the most important concepts, I reduced the total number to eight, which enabled me to focus better on the approach and outcome.

What a powerful lesson to learn early in my life! I started to call these most important concepts MegaCepts, and this has significantly and positively impacted my life ever since.

I began applying my new process—the MegaCepts process—in all my college courses. I started receiving good grades on the physics quizzes and in all my other courses during my four years in college. I graduated with a Bachelor of Science in Engineering degree with a four-year grade average of A-, even though my classes and labs took up twenty-eight hours per week.

In addition to the classes and labs, I also played two varsity sports: football and baseball. Believe it or not, I even used the MegaCepts process to become a better tailback in football. Our football rules, techniques, and playbook were over 125 pages and very detailed. I found the most important parts by applying the

MegaCepts process. For example, the playbook detailed over one hundred plays, but I found that only five were used 80 percent of the time. So, I focused on being the best on those plays.

I began using the MegaCepts process in college, and I have continued to use this helpful thinking and decision-making process in every aspect of my life.

My first job after college in 1967 was at IBM during their explosive growth in the 1960s, riding the company's leadership in the computer revolution. IBM's CEO, Thomas J. Watson Sr., had made the company's signature theme "THINK."

THINK signs were everywhere, encouraging all employees to think about everything they could do to make the company and its products better. His famous quote is, "Thought has been the father of every advance since time began." There is no question that IBM's THINK theme was instrumental in its rise to become one of the most successful companies in the world for many decades. And there is no question in my mind that better thinking is facilitated by focusing on the MegaCepts—the greatest thoughts—of all topics!

After IBM, I became a start-up company entrepreneur and leader in the explosive technology world of Silicon Valley, California. That world was, and still is, complex, fast moving, competitive, and dynamic—the perfect environment to apply the power of focusing on the greatest thoughts of any given subject. It was through this work that I further developed the MegaCepts process that is the core of this book while working and leading others as:

- **CEO of four technology companies:** A successful CEO must constantly think about the company situation and the best decisions to ensure the best business results. I always focused on the MegaCepts—the greatest thoughts—in these areas for each company, and this was critical to my success. This was my on-the-job-training approach to developing and applying the MegaCepts process.

- **Strategic advisor and coach:** I have acted in this capacity for dozens of CEOs and hundreds of leaders of other technology companies. I have used and taught the MegaCepts process to provide the best guidance and focus for each company's CEO, other leaders, and members of the board of directors.

- **A member of the board of directors for a dozen companies:** Board members have a legal and fiduciary obligation to do what is in the best interests of the shareholders. This requires careful, objective thought on the key strategic and policy matters of the company. I applied—and coached the other board members to apply—MegaCepts in the decision-making process as the most effective way to consistently perform this obligation.

- **A board member and trustee of multiple nonprofit institutions:** Most nonprofit boards have many trustees as board members. One institution focuses on the history of the information age, and at this institution I am one of over forty trustees on the board. Constantly thinking about and refining the MegaCepts—the greatest concepts—of the information age has been incredibly valuable to me in my trustee roles. It has also helped focus the thinking of a diverse group of trustees.

Structured thinking, as epitomized by the MegaCepts process, is a powerful way to get such a diverse group of people to make decisions on a consensus basis.

- **A venture capital investor in dozens of new, innovative companies:** One of the keys to smart investing is carefully defining the top "investment thesis" points for making the investment. My investment teams and I consistently used the MegaCepts process to better think through the key investment thesis points for each investment we made or did *not* make!

I want to provide you with a specific example of how I applied the MegaCepts process to one of my career activities. When I was acting as the executive chairman of a new start-up company in the educational technology (EdTech) software market, I was asked to advise the CEO and board of directors of the company on the key principles for how we could raise $10 million of venture capital (VC). So, I used the MegaCepts process to answer the question, "What are the most important factors that a VC will consider in making an investment in this company?"

I won't take you through my entire process, but I do want to share the final greatest thoughts with you. You don't need to understand the specifics of this EdTech software company, but this example will give you an understanding of what a final list of MegaCepts—the greatest thoughts on this topic—might look like. The company's CEO and board of directors adopted and moved forward with this list.

- **EdTech software company funding review:** Rank ordered the most important factors for VCs to invest $10 million.

- **Leadership team:** Passionate and driven to succeed with excellent EdTech market knowledge. Strong software R&D/product experience.

- **Market:** Large and rapidly growing total available market (TAM) and served available market (SAM), both in terms of the number of K–12 schools, administrators, teachers, students, and parents as well as associated potential returns based on reasonable pricing assumptions. Strong strategic interest in and high value from executive functioning skills (EFS).

- **Product/technology:** Innovative, new EFS features/functions/capabilities. Strong software R&D and development capability to maintain product leadership.

- **Competition:** New and differentiated EFS value proposition. High barriers to entry for new competitors.

- **Go-to-market (GTM):** Differentiated target market focus. Leveraged direct and indirect sales channels.

- **Strategic partners (SPs):** Potentially large number of relevant SP targets. Focused SP potential with current EdTech software platform companies.

- **Revenue model:** Above market growth rate. High recurring and repeat revenue.

- **Financials:** Good gross margin and pretax profit at reasonable revenue levels. Early achievement of positive cash flow to reduce future equity capital requirements.

- **Investment/funding model:** Reasonable level of equity capital is required to achieve success. Total funding requirement of $12 million to achieve positive cash flow.

- **Liquidity:** Reasonably large number of merger-and-acquisition candidates. Attractive financial growth and profitability to achieve high acquisition multiples.

The company used this MegaCepts list to produce its investor collateral, such as an investor email summary and executive summary. And they used this list as an outline to build their slide deck. For example, the first two slides in the deck provided bios of the leadership team that focused on their extensive EdTech knowledge and software development expertise.

The good news is that this structured way to think about a topic, in this case VC funding, produced a successful approach and process that resulted in funding success.

Look back for a minute at the above MegaCepts list. Take a mental picture of it, because it is the fairly typical result of applying the MegaCepts process. In this case, the list includes ten MegaCepts, which should be the limit. Each of the MegaCepts can have one or more sub-definers that further clarify the MegaCepts. The entire list is about one letter-sized page long, and you should try to keep your own MegaCepts lists to about the same length. You will learn the step-by-step MegaCepts process and see more examples of MegaCepts lists in this book.

Applying the MegaCepts process has also benefitted me in my personal life in many ways, including in the following areas:

- **Family issues:** How to discuss, understand, or solve them.

- **Friends' and associates' issues:** How to discuss, understand, or help them solve them.

- **Financial plans and needs:** How to understand and best manage my personal and family financial affairs.

- **Personal and family health:** How to understand and best manage my physical and mental health and well-being.

In short, the MegaCepts process has the potential to help you achieve more well-being and success in all areas of your personal and professional life.

Key Themes of This Book

- **Thinking is for everyone:** You don't have to be a genius to think better and more effectively, but you do need to commit to it and then have a simple and easy-to-use process to help facilitate your thinking.

- **Thinking should be focused:** This book proves that all subjects, from the simplest to the most complex, can be broken down into ten or fewer greatest thoughts, or MegaCepts.

- **Thinking can be easy:** This book provides an easy-to-learn, four-step process that anyone can use to better understand any subject, resulting in dramatically better thinking and the resulting benefits from that thinking. This process is illustrated with several real-life examples in this book.

- **Thinking by using the MegaCepts process works:** I have been successfully using and teaching the MegaCepts process for over five decades with many positive results.

You do not have to be a genius to think better. You just need to apply a logical and structured process. Applying the MegaCepts process to all aspects of your life is simple, easy, and powerful, but you must actually do it.

This book will help you do it. In keeping with the MegaCepts theme, this book is short and to the point. You will learn how to better think about, understand, and manage any topic in your life, which will result in expanded education and learning, enhanced understanding and knowledge, reinforced confidence, strengthened leadership skills, and increased happiness and fulfillment.

Read on, and as you do, think in a focused and intense way about everything you are reading. If you read something without thinking about it, chances are you won't understand it or retain it, so make a commitment to read and think in a focused, intense way.

"Very little is needed to make a happy life; it is all within yourself, in your way of thinking."

—MARCUS AURELIUS

CHAPTER 2

Apply the MegaCepts Process to Clarify the Greatest Thoughts on Any Topic

"I think, therefore I am."

—RENE DESCARTES

W e live in a complex world that is growing ever more complicated. Complexity exists at a macro, worldwide level when we deal with issues such as world hunger or controlling nuclear weapons, and it also occurs at a micro, personal level when we ponder how to make ends meet or be good parents.

With the ubiquitous spread of computers, the internet, search engines, artificial intelligence, and the associated information sources, an immense amount of data is available on virtually any topic. Compare this to fifty years ago when the primary source of information on a specific topic was the encyclopedia, a handful of books, or a news program. However, this explosion of information can be like drinking water from a firehose—you can drown in it without really understanding what you need to know.

Even well-organized encyclopedic sources, such as Wikipedia, can give us information overload. For example, the Wikipedia article discussing the topic of gravity is over seventy pages long with tens of thousands of words, including the many reference links to learn more. As you will learn in this book, the MegaCepts process is a simpler, more powerful way to understand any other topic in the world.

The MegaCepts process provides a structured way to deal with the complexity and information overload around us. Specifically, what are MegaCepts? I coined this word myself. It is derived from *mega*, which is Greek for "great or greatest, or mighty or mightiest." And *cepts*, which is short for "concepts, or thoughts and ideas."

As you read in Chapter 1, MegaCepts are the ten or fewer greatest thoughts on any given topic. This doesn't suggest that there aren't other concepts, thoughts, ideas, and principles that have value on a given topic. However, it does mean that if you can effectively define the greatest thoughts on a topic, you will be able to think more clearly about that topic and understand it in the most effective way possible.

The key to finding the greatest thoughts on a topic is to force yourself to really consider what the most important ten or fewer concepts might be. This means taking a few minutes to rank order them from most important to least important. The MegaCepts process will provide you with a structured approach to establish the true greatest thoughts on any topic, as opposed to just a loose grouping of some basic concepts and ideas. Once you learn this easy process and apply it to a few topics of interest, you will see the difference.

Authors of articles, books, and research papers universally use this general approach when summarizing the most important points on a topic. While such authors may not necessarily create MegaCepts, as we have defined them (ten or fewer greatest thoughts on the topic), they do regularly work to distill the most important points on a given topic. For example, you will frequently come across articles summarizing the top five-to-ten most important points regarding subjects such as:

- Causes of car accidents
- Reasons why people become obese
- Ways to become a better student
- Approaches to achieving better health

Authors who are experts on a topic often establish major points such as these, and you can use this simple MegaCepts process to do the same, but even better. Clarifying the greatest thoughts on a topic can help you think effectively about any problem, goal, or subject you'd like to understand better and make better leadership decisions.

You may be skeptical about the idea that any topic, including complex ones, can be defined by ten or fewer greatest thoughts. I have had over fifty years of experience defining MegaCepts for all my own most important topics. I have coached hundreds of leaders to do the same. I have also researched many other important subjects to identify their greatest thoughts. My personal and coaching experience as well as my research have confirmed the validity of the MegaCepts approach to great thinking and leadership decision-making.

Let me demonstrate how the MegaCepts process can lend great clarity to three important and complex subjects: religion, government, and science. Each has its own greatest thoughts, or MegaCepts, that provide a valuable framework or context for great thinking about each one.

Religion

- There are seven major religions in the world.

- Each of these has ten or fewer greatest thoughts defined by its ultimate authorities. Here are a few examples:

    - Christianity and Judaism: The Ten Commandments

    - Buddhism: The Four Noble Truths and Five Precepts

- Islam: The Six Articles of Faith

- In just a bit, I will use Christianity as an example. Appendix 3 contains the MegaCepts and additional interesting information for six of the other seven major world religions: Buddhism, Confucianism, Hinduism, Islam, Judaism, and Taoism. Read this appendix if you want more proof that each religion has its own greatest thoughts or if you are interested in learning more about these religions and comparing them.

Government

- There are eight major government types in the world.

- Each of these has ten or fewer greatest thoughts, or MegaCepts, defined by its ultimate authorities. For example:

  - Democratic republics, such as the United States: The original seven Articles of the Constitution and ten Amendments to the Constitution, called the Bill of Rights

  - Communism: The four Principles of the *Communist Manifesto* and the ten goals of the Communist Party

- Appendix 4 contains the greatest thoughts for the eight major government forms including anarchy, communism, democracy, monarchy, oligarchy, socialism, theocracy, and totalitarianism. Read this appendix if you want more proof that each government type has its own greatest thoughts or if you are interested in comparing these eight most prevalent forms of government.

Science

- There are three major branches of science:

  - The physical sciences: The study of nonliving systems

  - The earth sciences: The study of the planet Earth

  - The life sciences: The study of living organisms, such as plants, animals, and human beings

- Each of these has ten or fewer greatest thoughts, or MegaCepts, defined by their ultimate authorities. Here are some examples:

  - Physical sciences: Three major subsegments including physics, which has five major laws

  - Earth sciences: Six major subsegments

Let's highlight the powerful benefits of the MegaCepts process using Christianity as an example. The primary book on Christianity is obviously the Bible, which contains sixty-six books. In addition, over one thousand other books have been written about Christianity. The Wikipedia article on Christianity is over thirty pages long with hundreds of separate research references. All of this makes thinking about Christianity extremely complex and daunting.

However, if you first study and think about the Ten Commandments and adopt them as the MegaCepts of Christianity, your ability to think about and understand Christianity improves dramatically. Let's list the Ten Commandments here (as presented on the website www.BibleInfo.com):

- You shall have no other gods before me.
- You shall make no idols.
- You shall not take the Lord's name in vain.
- Keep the Sabbath day holy.
- Honor your father and your mother.
- You shall not murder.
- You shall not commit adultery.
- You shall not steal.
- You shall not bear false witness against thy neighbor.
- You shall not covet.

If you think about these and accept them as the greatest thoughts about Christianity, the MegaCepts, you will be better able to think about and understand everything else you read, study, and discuss about Christianity.

If you research each of these ideas separately, you will find further clarification. For example, if you search for information on the second commandment, you will find variations of the following, such as this Biblical quotation on www.BibleInfo.com: "You shall not make for yourself a carved image—any likeness of anything that is in heaven above, or that is in the earth beneath, or that is in the water under the earth; You shall not bow down to them, nor serve them: for I the LORD your God am a jealous God, visiting the inequity of the fathers upon the children to the third and fourth generation of them that hate me; but showing mercy to thousands to them that love me, and keep my Commandments."

Once you are comfortable with the validity of the idea and the power behind MegaCepts, the next step is to understand the MegaCepts process, so you can use it to establish the MegaCepts for any topic that is personally or professionally of interest to you. As illustrated above, some important topics come with predefined greatest thoughts supplied by authorities. But many more topics do not have predefined greatest thoughts, and that's when you will need to think about and establish your own.

An Overview of the Four-Step MegaCepts Process

The MegaCepts process provides a step-by-step approach to establish the most relevant greatest thoughts on different topics. As a reminder, while you can apply the MegaCepts process to think about virtually any topic under the sun (such as gravity), the process has the most impact and power when you apply it in your personal and professional life. The process has four steps:

1. **Initial ideas:** Write down what you think are the most important concepts of a specific topic that you want to learn more about, especially if you need to make a decision on the topic. This step is essential, since it motivates and

disciplines you to capture your initial thoughts on a topic before seeking input from others. This step reflects the starting point, or baseline, in your thinking about the topic. It's useful and enlightening to compare your initial ideas to your final MegaCepts list.

2. **Socialized ideas:** Without sharing your work, ask two or three friends, family members, or associates to offer their most important concepts on the topic. Once you discuss the topic with two or three other people, you will all understand it much better.

3. **Research ideas:** Once you have established your own ideas and socialized ideas, complement these with focused, high-level research. Do an internet search for articles and research that deal specifically with your topic.

4. **Your MegaCepts List:** Based on your initial ideas, the social input you received, and your further research, go back to your list and refine it to establish your own greatest thoughts on the topic, your MegaCepts. This final step in the process will provide a surprising amount of insight and clarity!

The key to the MegaCepts process is that it facilitates and emphasizes your ability to think about and process information rather than just read or hear information and then simply remember it. As you learn more about the process, you will understand how it positively forces you to think.

Thinking—the heart of the MegaCepts process—is one of the most important human capabilities in life for all individuals in every facet of our society including, of course, all governments and institutions. However, most people do not think effectively and, in many cases, do not think at all. That is, we repeat what we read or hear. This lack of thinking negatively impacts our success, happiness, and fulfillment.

People who think effectively generally do it in a more organized and structured way, and the MegaCepts process provides a powerful way to accomplish that, from the simplest topics and subjects to the most complex. You will find that:

- Great thinking, which enables better leadership decision-making, produces more successful, happier, and fulfilled people.

- Applying the principles of this book will lead to this great thinking and better leadership decision-making.

Hundreds of books have been written about thinking over the ages. Appendix 2 briefly profiles twenty-four modern-day books in the following five categories:

- **Major types of thinking:** Books in this category explain how to think via the seven major types of thinking: critical, analytical, creative, abstract, concrete, convergent, and divergent.

- **Organized thinking:** These books teach how to think using organized and structured techniques.

- **Life impacts of thinking:** These books show how thinking impacts our lives in ways such as happiness, education, success, and fulfillment.

- **Group thinking:** This category of books offers practical guidance to improve the collective thinking for groups and teams of people working together.

- **Business and professional thinking:** These books present structured operational, tactical, and strategic thinking approaches applied to the complex challenges of running an enterprise.

I have reviewed all twenty-four of these books and believe they all contribute, in different ways, to getting people to think more effectively in their respective areas of focus. However, I also believe thinking better requires a more practical, understandable, and easy-to-use approach, and that's what this *Mega Thinking* book and the MegaCepts process provides. The four clear steps presented above empower you to think more clearly and to better understand any topic. MegaCepts is a universal way to think about any topic, including other thinking books. The four process steps are simple and easy to understand. Later chapters illustrate the process steps with six stories of real people successfully applying the MegaCepts process to a diverse set of topics.

Once you learn the MegaCepts process, you'll discover ample opportunities in your professional and personal life to apply this simple, easy, and powerful approach to thinking and decision-making. I truly believe this process will empower you to think smarter and make better leadership decisions.

"To find yourself, think for yourself."

—SOCRATES

CHAPTER 3

THINKING ABOUT THINKING:
How Great Thinking Impacts Our Lives and Leadership Decisions

"We are what we think."

—GAUTAMA BUDDHA

Before we dive more deeply into the MegaCepts process, let's take a brief step back to think a little bit more about thinking itself. Many believe that thinking is the most important activity we can do, with the greatest impact on our lives.

One way to describe the human thinking process is to explain it in the same way experts describe how a computer works. We have seen incredible advances in computing in the last few decades, but despite this computing revolution, the original computing model is still valid. So, as simple as it sounds, it is applicable and enduring. Computers are made up of four basic "parts":

1. **Input:** This is the raw data that is fed into a computer on a given subject or topic via multiple devices and sources.

2. **Process/processing:** A computer analyzes, processes, and "thinks about" the input by employing powerful software programs that provide the logic for this process. The computer is always "thinking" logically, in a highly organized and structured way!

3. **Storage/memory:** This is where the computer stores temporary (memory) or permanent (storage) answers, analyses, conclusions, and so forth.

4. **Output:** The computer provides output in many forms and at any time it is asked to do so.

Given the incredible impact of the computer and the information revolution, this may seem overly simplistic. But even though it is a simple model, it is also powerful and valid. As you read this book, you will learn how to apply an analogous model that is simple and powerful for thinking smarter: the MegaCepts process.

The important concept here is that the human brain works in much the same way as the computing model, as shown in Figure 1.

1. **Input:** This is the "raw" data, facts, and information that is fed into the brain on many different subjects and topics, via multiple sources, including seeing, hearing, smelling, tasting, and touching.

2. **Process/processing:** The brain analyzes, processes, and thinks about the input. Some of this is subconscious, such as when the brain regulates your breathing and heartbeat. Some of it is conscious for simple "processes," such as showering and getting dressed. And some of it is conscious and involves more sophisticated thinking on more complex subjects, such as the study of physics or how to be a good parent. The brain is always "thinking" logically in a very organized and structured way for subconscious and simple conscious processes and topics. But very often, the brain is not applied to more complex subjects in an organized and structured way. It can use some help here, and that help can come directly from the person who has the brain!

3. **Storage/memory:** This is where you store temporary and permanent answers, analyses, conclusions, facts, and

so forth. Your brain has an extremely large storage and memory capacity.

4. **Output:** The brain provides output in many forms and at any time it is asked to do so. Many times, this is done subconsciously, or it is done consciously for simple subjects or processes. Many times, on more complex subjects, the brain simply provides output that was stored in the memory but was not processed or thought about. The key to more intelligent output is to think—really think, in a logical and structured manner—before simply "dumping your memory."

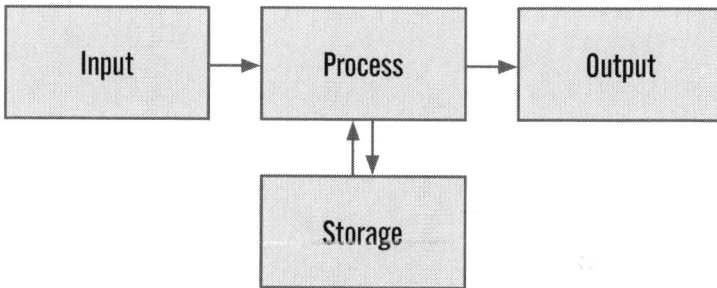

Figure 1: The human brain and computer both "think" in much the same way!

If applied properly, your brain has thousands of times more processing (thinking) power than a computer. For example, consider that developmental psychologist Howard Gardner identified nine different types of intelligence: verbal, logical, visual, kinesthetic, musical, interpersonal, intrapersonal, naturalist, and existential. We could list many other examples of the brain's power, but it is sufficient to say that your brain, and its ability to think, is far more sophisticated than the most powerful computers.

However, to achieve the incredible power of thinking that your brain possesses, you need to do the following:

1. Commit to thinking versus repeating what you stored away in your memory from the "raw" input you received.

2. Apply a disciplined, structured, and organized approach to thinking.

This is a simple but important point that is worth illustrating with an example. Two students are in a high school history class, and the current focus is World War II. The teacher gives the following assignment:

-   Read *The Rise and Fall of the Third Reich: A History of Nazi Germany* by William L. Shirer.

-   Write a report explaining what the book says about why Germany took certain actions that led to World War II.

-   Focus on *why* Nazi Germany did what it did, not just *what* it did.

The first student read the book and took good notes on all the major events. He wrote his report focusing on some of those events, such as:

- Hitler's rise to power starting in 1933

- Germany's invasion of Poland in 1939

- Germany's opening of an eastern front in the war with Russia

His report was strong on what happened but weak on why these events happened. Essentially, his input, memory, and output were all good, but his processing (thinking) was limited, based on the teacher's assignment.

The second student also read the book and took good notes on all the major events. However, for each of the events, he wrote down the book's explanations as the root cause or causes. He then wrote his report focusing on some of those events and the causes, such as:

- Hitler's rise to power, starting in 1933, was primarily due to the Nazi Party's commitment to the German people and its hope to restore the country as a world power after its defeat in World War I.

- Part of the restoration plan was to expand the German empire to include surrounding Germanic nations, such as Poland and Austria.

- Germany's opening of an eastern front in the war with Russia was an offensive move to stop the Russians from preventing Germany's invasion of other countries.

So, the second student really thought about how to answer the *why* part of the assignment. His input, memory, and output were all good and so was his processing (thinking), based on the teacher's assignment.

The first student would probably receive a C on his report, because he simply recorded a few key events highlighted in the book and did not address the teacher's instruction to discuss *why* Nazi Germany did what it did. The second student would most likely receive an A, because he really thought about the question and provided those thoughts as his answers. This is an example of thinking smarter for a better life, or in this case, for a better test score.

I believe great thinking has at least four important impacts on our lives and two key requirements:

- **Thinking defines us:** Thinking is an innate capability of mankind. If properly applied (or not), it is a primary factor in defining who we are.

- **Thinking educates us:** Improved thinking is also learning, which leads to better knowledge and wisdom on any topic. This is especially true for more challenging and complex topics and issues.

- **Thinking impacts our success:** Your ability to think, and your actual application of thinking, will have a major impact on your success or failure in all aspects of your life, including personally, educationally, and professionally.

- **Thinking has other personal benefits:** Thinking provides other mental and emotional benefits, including higher confidence, better self-image, more complete self-fulfillment, and even increased happiness. Better thinking helps you to get on top of any topic and to manage it effectively.

- **Thinking requires you to actively and effectively use your brain:** Many—perhaps most—people do not think as much as they should and could. Many literally don't think at all about complex topics. Even those who do think often think less effectively than they are capable of thinking. You need to turn your brain on, just like you need to turn your computer on.

- **Thinking needs commitment and discipline:** Thinking might seem complex and intimidating, but it doesn't have to be. You can learn to think better, but you need to desire that goal, and you need to apply yourself. Applying an organized and structured way to think is the best way to think better about any topic.

There are literally thousands of famous quotations on thinking from a wide array of philosophers, religious leaders, and authors, recorded through the centuries. I have selected ninety-nine of these to show how thinking impacts the above six areas. I have also included a seventh category to highlight some quotations about thinking that are particularly witty, fun, and satirical. Many of these quotations are included in the main portion of this book, and you will find all ninety-nine in Appendix 1.

Exercise

Before we get into the step-by-step details to learn and practice the MegaCepts process, I want to leave you with a short exercise. Jot down your answers to the questions below in a physical notebook, on your phone, or in a computer file. It doesn't matter where you put the document, but keep it safe, and don't share it with anyone. Your answers will provide you with personal guidance on what is most important to you about thinking before you read the rest of this book. After you have read this book, we will come back to these questions again to see how your answers have changed.

- How important do you believe that thinking is in your life today?

- How much more important would you like it to be for you in the future?

- How would you rate yourself on how often and how well you think today?

- How important is it that you learn to think more and think better?

———o————o———

"The happiness of your life depends
on the quality of your thoughts."

—MARCUS AURELIUS

———o————o———

CHAPTER 4

Learn and Practice the Simple, Four-Step MegaCepts Process

"Principles and rules are intended to provide a thinking man with a frame of reference."

—KARL VON CLAUSEWITZ

This chapter explains the step-by-step MegaCepts process, which you can apply to any topic you'd like to think about more effectively, particularly if you need to make a decision about that topic.

Step 1: Your Initial Ideas

Everyone has initial ideas about any topic without having researched anything first. Therefore, formally capturing your initial ideas is the critical starting point for the MegaCepts process.

It is important to pick a topic that you really want to know more about, not just a topic that you think will make you look smart to someone else. You should formally state the topic as clearly and concisely as you can. For example, you might state the topic as, "How can I become the best parent for my teenage children?"

Take a moment to think about a topic that you'd like to learn more about. This topic could relate to your personal or professional life. You may want to select a subject that is currently on your mind, for example, perhaps you have been asked to take on new responsibilities at work or a new role in a community organization, and you need to make an informed decision.

As soon as you think about your initial ideas, jot them down, and then think a little more about them. Once you have written down your initial ideas, a valuable next step is to study them and then rate yourself on how well you think you understand the topic. Use a scale of one to ten, with one meaning little or no understanding and ten meaning the very highest level of understanding.

Rate yourself in the following five categories:

- Education on the topic
- Understanding of the topic
- Confidence about the topic
- Ability to provide leadership on the topic
- Current satisfaction regarding the topic

Step 2: Socialized Ideas

Asking others for their thoughts about the key concepts on a topic is a highly valuable next step. So, choose two or three friends, family members, or colleagues to help you. Start by asking them for their thoughts before you share yours. You will all learn a lot from this step. It is important to pick people who may have relevant knowledge and whom you trust to honestly communicate their thoughts on the topic.

The best way to get the highest quality of thinking from this step is to ask them to think about the topic and then meet with them individually to hear their thoughts. After getting their ideas, share your initial thoughts and discuss each thought to learn more.

After you have met with two or three people and kept good notes, you should rethink your original ideas while factoring in their input. This will produce your socialized understanding of the topic, which will be more thoughtful and better than your initial ideas. In fact, this may be a surprisingly eye-opening experience—possibly the first of many in this process!

Step 3: Research Ideas

To understand a topic, many people would begin here. However, in the MegaCepts process, the research step builds on the prior two steps, and it is driven by thought. Really think about the gaps in your socialized ideas. In this step, search for articles that specifically address any gaps or questions you might have, and search for articles that most directly address your topic.

For example, if you are researching how to become a better parent of teenagers, you might type in a search phrase like, "Top 10 most important ways to parent a teenager."

Once you have selected the most useful and relevant thoughts from your research, write them down and think about which ones you believe are the most important.

Step 4: Your MegaCepts List

You are now ready to establish your final thoughts on the subject, resulting in your greatest thoughts. This final step requires a lot of careful thought on your part to take the multiple inputs and synthesize them into your best thoughts on the topic. You should ask yourself which points are the most important and why. You should then rank order them using your best judgment and starting with the most important. Once this list is finalized, you should rate yourself again on your understanding of the topic. I assure you that if you effectively implement this four-step process, your score from step one will improve dramatically.

Although this is a final list of MegaCepts on the subject, you should view it as the first major step in a continuous process to refine your thinking about and understanding of the topic. Make it your own, believed-in list. Keep it in your mind and, as appropriate, put copies of it in front of you constantly, such as on a bathroom mirror, refrigerator door, bulletin board, and cell phone list. Every chance you get, continue to discuss your MegaCepts on this topic with anyone who might be interested and have relevant information to contribute.

The next six chapters show, step-by-step, how six people applied the MegaCepts process to six important topics. In each case they used the process to think smarter about their topic to arrive at ten or fewer greatest thoughts that will guide their leadership decision-making on each topic in the future. The subjects include personal, educational, and professional topics, since all these need great thinking and better leadership decision-making.

Each of the following six examples is quite different and adds value, helping you further understand how you can practice using the MegaCepts process in both your personal and professional life. I like to keep in mind that leadership, decision-making, and great thinking apply to every aspect of our multifaceted lives—at work, at home, and when volunteering for our community or house of worship. As I noted in the first chapter, the ability to make better personal and professional leadership decisions leads to a better, more fulfilling, and successful life.

Chapters 5 and 6 illustrate how anyone can use this process for any topic. The two real-life examples include a mother who stepped through the MegaCepts process to gain a better understanding of how to be a better parent to her two teenage children and a student who used the process to better understand the ramifications of his choice of college major.

Chapters 7 and 8 illustrate how two professionals used the process to study specific topics in more depth. Chapter 7 tells the story of a technology professional who used the MegaCepts process to better understand interpersonal skills and ultimately improve his chances of becoming a manager. Chapter 8 relates the experience of a marketing professional who considered a career change to artificial intelligence and applied the MegaCepts process to become more knowledgeable in that field and improve his networking ability.

Chapters 9 and 10 discuss how even very knowledgeable experts in their fields can benefit from using the MegaCepts process to further hone their knowledge with better, more structured thinking. The two real-life examples include a business leader who applied the process to become an even better leader and a medical expert who sought to improve healthcare by reducing medical errors.

As you read these real-life experiences, think about how each person applied the MegaCepts process and how the resulting MegaCepts list, their greatest thoughts, will empower them to make better leadership decisions related to their topic. Also, think about how their resulting greatest thoughts lists help *you* better understand their topics.

I have provided short exercises after Chapter 6, Chapter 8, and Chapter 10, so you can practice the MegaCepts process. As you read the next chapters, I hope you will discover that *thinking about thinking* is both fun and rewarding!

*"I cannot teach anybody anything,
I can only make them think."*

—SOCRATES

CHAPTER 5

Applying the MegaCepts Process to Become a Better Parent

"Dare to think for yourself."

—VOLTAIRE

Jane is a successful person. She is a spouse, career professional, and mother of two children. She felt that she was a very good mother as her children were growing up. When they reached ten and twelve years old, she (and her husband) started thinking about how to be the best parent possible when her children become teenagers. Being a good parent to teenagers is often perceived as the most challenging period of parenthood.

Jane is blessed to have many friends at different socio-economic, age, and parental-stage levels. She had been thinking about parenting challenges when her children would become teenagers and had been asking her friends about their experiences being a parent to teenagers. She was amazed at the input and reactions she received. She told me, "It is almost like all parents of teenagers have had common experiences." She recorded and shared these comments from her friends:

Cherry: "I know I'm supposed to be preparing my teenager for life, but it's hard when they already know everything!"

Steve: "The scariest part of raising teenagers is remembering the stupid things I did as a teenager."

Christy: I used to worry a lot when my kids were little. Then I had teenagers. You know what I would give right now to worry about sippy cups and napping? Everything!"

With the above as context, Jane felt a strong desire to think about and understand how to be a great mother during her children's teenage years. After learning about the MegaCepts process, she wanted to apply it to learn how she could be a better parent to her teenagers. So, Jane defined her topic as, "How can I be the best parent possible for my two teenage children?"

Here's what she said about the MegaCepts process before starting the process: "I liked that it encouraged me to develop my own thoughts about the topic before I sought others' ideas. I also liked that it focused me to find the ten or fewer most important ideas about the topic." Before starting the process, she rated herself on the topic as follows on a scale of one to ten:

- Education on the topic: 2
- Understanding of the topic: 4
- Confidence about the topic: 3
- Ability to provide leadership on the topic: 3
- Current satisfaction regarding the topic: 2
- Total score: 14

Jane felt she did not have a lot of formal education regarding parenting teenagers. This is typical when anyone thinks about a new topic. Her understanding of the topic was higher in large part, since she believed her successful parenting of preteen children gave her some "going in" ideas, as reflected in her initial ideas below. The confidence and leadership scores correspond to her prior two scores. Her low satisfaction score (fourteen points out of a possible fifty points) reflects her strong desire and commitment to think about and learn more about being the best parent she can be to her teenagers.

When you start to think seriously about any topic, such as parenting, it is healthy and objective to start the thinking process with an open mind, and that is exactly what Jane did.

Step 1: Jane's Initial Ideas

She started by writing down her best thoughts on the topic and then revising them a few more times over the course of a day or so:

- Give your children unqualified love, so they know they are safe and secure under your care.

- Clearly define the most important rules you expect them to follow.

- Teach them the importance of being honest, ethical, and moral.

- Give them as much independence as possible.

Her first three ideas were basically the same ones that she and her husband had used in raising their young children. The fourth idea was based on the understanding she'd gained from friends that teenagers need less parental dependence and more personal independence.

As she looked at these initial ideas, she felt comfortable that all four were important to being a good parent to teenagers. However, for each idea, she wondered how different it would be to implement it with a teenager. Giving unqualified love to an eight-year-old is relatively easy since, at that age, the child wants and needs that love and attention. Providing unqualified love to a sixteen-year-old would require a very different approach. This is part of what Jane wanted to learn from the next two steps in the MegaCepts process: socializing her ideas with her friends and doing some focused research.

Step 2: Jane's Socialized Ideas

Jane reached out to two friends to get their thoughts on this important topic. She wanted to get input from both a mother and a father's point of view. She also wanted input from a current parent of teenagers who would be able to provide "real-time" thoughts and from a parent of adult children who would be able to provide "hindsight is twenty-twenty" thoughts. She found those qualities in her friends Sandy and Ken.

In both cases, Jane asked for their initial, unguided thoughts on the topic of how to be the best parent possible when your children become teenagers. Then she asked them questions about her ideas on the topic and about their ideas. Through this part of the process, both friends provided her with a total of nineteen inputs, some of which overlapped with her original list. The most important new thoughts on the topic were the following:

- **Organize regular and quality time together:** This is easy when your children are young but much more difficult when they are teenagers.

- **Teach them to respect authority:** This is often a challenge due to teenagers wanting to make their own rules.

- **Encourage extracurricular activities:** This helps build a teenager's confidence and provides some life balance and socialization skills.

- **Help build their self-confidence in other ways:** This includes justified praise, reinforcing their independent thinking, and so forth.

As she continued to socialize the topic with her friends, she further defined and detailed her list. I found it interesting that each of the three parents involved with this process left feeling smarter about the topic. Clearly, there is a huge thinking advantage for those who openly discuss a topic.

One of her friends ended the discussion with Jane by sharing the following wisdom, which she claimed to be part of her "parents of teenagers" lore: "Raising a teenager is hard, but being a teenager is hard, too, which is why our kids need someone they trust to lean on, to come to for advice, and to share their lives with—the good, the bad, and the ugly. Having a front-row seat in our kids' lives is far better than sitting in the nosebleed seats."

Step 3: Jane's Research Ideas

After capturing her own thoughts and then integrating the thoughts of her friends, Jane felt much more able to do some focused research on the topic. The socialization process was extremely valuable, since it provided her with new ideas to help clarify her initial ideas.

She focused her research on some key areas she wanted to further clarify, including the following: techniques for convincing teenagers to spend more time with their parents, ways to help teenagers balance independence with respect for others, approaches to help teenagers build their self-confidence, and ways to encourage a teenager to accept a parent's unqualified love.

Jane's initial ideas were primarily about what to do as the parent of teenagers. Her socialization step added additional "what's" but also started to focus on how to do them. The research step yielded her a few new "what's," but it was primarily focused on how to achieve those specific activities and behaviors.

She found two valuable articles, which were "Essential Tips for Positive Parenting Your Teen!" and "Parenting Teenagers: Discipline, Communication, and More." She wrote down the most important ideas from each article, with a focus on *how* to be a better parent for teenagers.

The first simple but powerful idea she embraced was using meals as a means to meet and communicate. She planned to prioritize eating meals together and periodically invite her children's friends to join a meal. To Jane, this seemed like a simple way to spend time together naturally, since everyone needs to eat.

This is just one form of family meeting that she discovered is important. Other family meetings can occur by linking them to activities and events such as sports, travel, cultural events, and holidays. One idea was to plan these family meetings together with your children, so they feel included in the process.

The second idea she really liked was that you don't have to be "just a parent" to your teenagers, you can also be a friend. You should parent actively and appropriately, but you should also be an active friend who simply enjoys spending time with your teenagers doing fun and rewarding activities. As both a parent and a friend, you can be a role model for your teenagers. For example, as a parent, you should act in a completely moral and ethical way, both to your children and other people. As a friend, you should treat your children and your other friends with respect and affection. Always keep your standards high, so they will hopefully do the same.

The third area she viewed as an extremely important "how" idea was focusing on communication. Keep the lines of communication humming. Always keep the communication door open. Question teenagers and listen to them before you rush to judgment, especially on important issues. Choose your battles wisely. Keep kids safe and connected to the family by keeping computers in your common space.

Another important idea was related to rules and discipline and adhering to the rules. Cleary establish some key rules, such as discussing and agreeing to "checking in," cleaning their rooms, helping with chores around the house, completing their homework on time, and so on. Parents should actively apply these rules, but when appropriate give teenagers some leeway, as no one at any age is perfect. Within the context of rules, give them independence, but don't push your teen into independence before they are ready.

Upon writing down and reviewing her research ideas on how to be a better parent to teenagers, Jane now felt more confident about how to integrate these ideas with her initial and socialized ideas to produce her own high-quality MegaCepts list.

Step 4: Jane's MegaCepts List

To formalize her own list of greatest thoughts on how to be the best parent to teenagers, Jane first reviewed her initial ideas and thought about what they had meant to her. She then reviewed the socialized ideas she had received in her discussions with her two friends. She realized the socialized ideas had significantly enhanced her initial ideas with new "what's" and some key "how's." Finally, she reviewed the research ideas, which were particularly helpful in further defining simple but powerful "how's."

Notice a few key points in Jane's list of nine greatest thoughts, below, versus her initial ideas. First, she added five new categories. Second, all nine of her greatest thoughts have better detail describing more about the particular MegaCepts. Finally, she included dramatically more ideas on how to achieve results for all the MegaCepts. For example, in the "Love, respect, and trust" bullet point in her MegaCepts list, she presents multiple ways to achieve that result.

Jane is confident these MegaCepts are the most important ideas on how to become the best mother she can be in raising her two teenage children. She intends to use these MegaCepts—her greatest thoughts on the topic—as a constant reminder of what she needs to do to be an effective parent. She will share this list with her husband, her children, and her friends.

- **Love, respect, and trust:** Give your children unqualified love, so they know they can trust you, believe you, and always talk with you about anything. Tell them you love them every day and show them affection. Build a trusting relationship with them and make them feel that it is safe to talk to you about any subject, including sex and teenage drinking. Praise them but also provide constructive criticism to help them learn and grow. Remember, you're a parent and a friend.

- **Regular and quality time together:** Establish dependable time together. Spend time as a family exchanging ideas and viewpoints. Eat family dinner together most nights, except when extracurricular activities conflict. This is a great time to bond as a family, share learning and experiences, and laugh together. Invite their friends to dinner. Hold family meetings on topics such as fixing up the house, where to go on vacation, and important family matters. Be a good listener. Remain calm in discussing controversial subjects. Use active listening when they discuss their concerns, fears, dreams, and hopes. Make them feel heard. Keep the lines of communication humming.

- **Independence and responsibility:** Give them independence. Allow them to make decisions on their own to develop this skill. Encourage them to make as many decisions for themselves as possible. Always give them your input but then suggest they take that input and make their own decisions. Ask for their input and opinions as well. Allow them to make mistakes. Talk through what they learned from their mistakes. Parent actively and appropriately. Give kids some leeway. Keep the door open.

- **Respect for authority:** Teach them to respect justified authority with parents, teachers, coaches, and law enforcement. Teach them manners, including table manners, respect for others, saying please and thank you, and so forth. Be a role model of good behavior.

- **Rules and discipline:** Cleary define the most important rules you expect them to follow around the house, at school, with friends, and in society. For example, discuss and agree to a "checking in" rule. Quickly point out when you feel they have admirably adhered to a rule and/or have disobeyed a rule. Choose your battles on these wisely, and don't battle over trivial rules or minor infractions.

- **Proper conduct:** Teach them the importance of being honest, ethical, and moral. Keep your standards high and be clear on each relevant point. Be a good role model for this.

- **Extracurricular activities:** Encourage and support extracurricular activities, such as sports, music, and art. Encourage them to try new activities to find out what they like and don't like. Ideally, these would include some that involve other people to promote interpersonal interaction and team involvement. Encourage participation in positive pursuits without forcing them to do these.

- **People and interpersonal skills:** Develop their understanding of and belief in the value of people in their lives and the associated benefits of strong interpersonal skills. Show empathy toward others, so they can learn to do the same. Identify activities that will develop their self-confidence and comfort around people, not only their peers but also adults.

- **Self-confidence:** Build their self-confidence and self-image, so they feel good "in their own skins." Praise them every time there is an opportunity, but don't give them false praise. Encourage them to find activities that develop their self-confidence. This could be anything from reading books on a favorite subject to participating in group activities.

After completing the MegaCepts process, Jane rated herself again on the topic:

- Education on the topic: 6
- Understanding of the topic: 8
- Confidence about the topic: 8
- Ability to provide leadership on the topic: 7
- Current satisfaction regarding the topic: 7
- Total score 36 versus 14 at the beginning of the process

Jane's score improvement is obviously significant in all areas. Her education and understanding scores increased due to the structured thinking process she used in each step. That dramatically increased her confidence and ability to lead on this topic. Her increase in confidence and leadership ability were also due to the fact that the process resulted in a specific set of MegaCepts. That specificity builds self-confidence and enables her to lead others. Driven by all these points, Jane's overall satisfaction level dramatically increased from two to seven. But as she admitted, "I'm not going to be completely satisfied until I achieve a ten rating; my teenagers are that important to me."

Jane now has a thoroughly developed list of greatest thoughts to help her be the best mother she can be for her teenage children. She has posted this list on her bathroom mirror, on the kitchen refrigerator, in her car, and in her office. She also has copies on her computer and smartphone.

Additionally, Jane has provided the list to her two children and discussed it in detail with them. They appreciated that their mother had completed this process to think about them. She knows she will be a much better mother due to these MegaCepts—her greatest thoughts on the topic—because she has developed her own structured way to think and then act effectively.

"The process made me focus and think about how to be a better mother," said Jane. "The resulting MegaCepts are something I have created and believe in. They are not just someone else's list. As a result, I have dramatically improved my understanding of, confidence in, and my ability to be a leader as a better mother. The entire process only took about nine hours, and I think the value of the result is worth a lot to me and my teenagers. And I actually had fun using the process to think!"

Brief Thoughts about Jane's MegaCepts Process and Parenting

Parenting is one of the most important activities in life. Good parenting of children results in happier, more stable, and successful lives for them. And that strengthens all of society. Jane's final MegaCepts list on how to be the best parent possible for teenagers is extremely well done. I had a similar list when I was a parent for my children, but Jane's list is better! And I plan to update my list to be the best grandparent I can be for my grandchildren.

I shared Jane's list with my daughter, who has two children, and she plans to use some of Jane's ideas as well. When I discussed this with my daughter, she made the somewhat tongue-in-cheek remark that the ideas can also be used with "parenting" older people when they start acting like teenagers, which she properly accuses me of doing from time to time!

"Whether you think you can or think you can't, you're right."

—HENRY FORD

CHAPTER 6

Applying the MegaCepts Process to Make an Important Educational Decision

"Those who think need no teachers."

—MAHATMA GANDHI

Today, a college education is a close second in importance to elementary and high school education. Between 2019 and 2021, 66.2 percent of all high school graduates went on to attend college. That is a dramatic increase over the past two hundred years. In 1800, only 1.1 percent of high school graduates went on to college. In 1900, that was 4.9 percent, and in 1950 it increased 15.1 percent.

So, pursuing a college education and then achieving professional success by applying that education is incredibly important. The obvious, most important first step is to do well in grades K–12, so you qualify to apply to college. The second important step is to apply to multiple colleges and be accepted at one or more that you find attractive. Once you attend college, it is important to choose your major while considering your interests and career aspirations.

In this chapter, we'll follow the story of John, the son of a close friend who used the MegaCepts process to choose a college major. While "choosing a college major" may not be on your current list of action items, this chapter presents a valuable example of applying the MegaCepts process to make an extremely important life decision.

John is bright and did well in K–12, both academically and in extracurricular activities. He applied to multiple colleges and got into several of them, including his "going in" favorite, which he then committed to attend. For several years, he had developed a strong interest in oceanography and marine biology. During his high school years, he worked during the summers at a marine mammal center. So, when he entered college, he chose biology as his major. In his freshman year of college, John also took a course in computer science and was struck by the importance of this field, both in general and in relation to other fields, such as biology.

As a rising sophomore, John wanted to clarify his thoughts on his future college major. He knew he had a deep interest in biology, but he was also intrigued by his newfound exposure to computer science. He wanted to investigate, think about, and understand computer science more deeply. Finally, he decided to use the MegaCepts process to answer the question, "Why is computer science relevant and important today, and what are the career opportunities?"

He rated himself on the topic as follows on a scale of one to ten:

- Education on the topic: 4
- Understanding of the topic: 4
- Confidence about the topic: 2
- Ability to provide leadership on the topic: 1
- Current satisfaction regarding the topic: 1
- Total score: 12

John felt he had some basic education and understanding of the subject from having used computers and the internet regularly and from taking the computer science course in his freshman year. But he gave his confidence in the topic and his ability to lead low scores, since he was now focused on computer science as an industry and career rather than simply using it. His low happiness regarding the topic was offset by his strong motivation to learn more, which was reflected by his low total score of twelve points (out of a possible fifty points). So, his self-assessment seemed to be objective and indicate a good mindset with which to start exploring the topic in more depth.

Step 1: John's Initial Ideas

His initial thoughts on the topic were:

- Technology that uses computers and software is common and is rapidly becoming pervasive in the world.

- Software engineers are in high demand for software development jobs.

- Software can be applied, along with hardware, to fix many of the world's issues.

- For many people, computing has become an important vehicle for socialization, communication, amusement, and education.

These initial ideas were fairly simple and influenced by his primary background as a user of personal computers and the internet. They were not based on computers as an industry or as a career. He wanted to learn much more about these latter areas in the next steps in the MegaCepts process.

Step 2: John's Socialized Ideas

John talked with his mom and dad, both of whom have careers in technology, and they provided their ideas about computers and computer science. John was particularly interested in getting their thoughts on key industry ideas, since he felt that was where he was weakest. He knew how to use computers fairly well, but he did not yet understand how computing impacts the world as an industry. His parents provided a number of ideas about the computer industry. He was particularly interested in the few that he deemed to be the most important new ideas to him. They included the following:

1. **The importance of computers to the world economy:** Computers now facilitate financial activity and the buying and selling of goods that drive the economy.

2. **The impact of computers on the information age:** Information is power, and computer science is needed to organize information in efficient ways and evaluate complicated data to make educated decisions.

3. **The significance of computing on science and research:** Computing is essential in contributing to scientific and research advances in fields like healthcare, agriculture, the environment, space exploration, and energy creation.

The last idea was the most important to John, since it reinforced the fact that any major field, such as biology, had been and will be significantly impacted by computers. This wasn't a total surprise to him, but based on his parent's emphasis of this, John would now make it one of the most important points to understand in more depth during the research step.

Step 3: John's Research Ideas

John did some high-level internet searches on the topic of computer science and found additional ideas that he listed. He then took that list, his original ideas, and the socialized ideas and found the most important new or reinforcing ideas to integrate.

First, he found a significant amount of information about artificial intelligence (AI). Experts now expect that computers will be intelligent and automated, so they can communicate and coordinate with people and each other. An example of this is Apple's Siri, a virtual assistant that can listen to commands and questions from people and respond intelligently, such as providing directions to a destination. Siri also communicates and coordinates with other computers and GPS devices.

Now, and even more in the future, many tasks that are done by people will be partially or completely done by computers. As John thought about this, his mind immediately turned to how this might impact biological research and other important areas. It was as if a light clicked on for him concerning just how integrated the fields of computer science and biology had become.

Second, the research provided him with additional ideas on the size and scope of the computer industry. It is the third largest industry in the world, behind healthcare and energy. It is the fastest-growing industry, which will make it the largest in the next couple of decades. It directly employs over 10 percent of the total workforce. It has significant impacts on all other industries. For many industries, such as internet-based retail, computers make it possible for them to exist.

Third, in his research, he spent a lot of time focusing on the importance of security. He was aware that security was important in certain areas such as using passwords and anti-spam protection, both of which he uses on his computer and when using the internet.

But he was amazed at just how important security is when it is characterized at the cybersecurity and potential cyber-war level.

John finished the socialized and research ideas steps with a much better understanding of the total computer industry in terms of its size and its influence on all other industries. He also gained a much better appreciation of the importance of security.

Step 4: John's MegaCepts List

John then produced the following integrated MegaCepts list on the topic of computer science:

- **Size and scope of the computer industry:** Technology that uses computers and software is common and is rapidly becoming pervasive in the world. Software can be applied along with hardware to address many of the world's issues.

- **Significant impact of computers on all other industries:** Software engineers in software development jobs are in high demand. This is especially true when software engineering is applied to key application areas, such as biological research and healthcare.

- **Significant impact of computers on society:** These impacts can be both beneficial and detrimental. For example, AI can be tremendously beneficial in treating medical patients more effectively. But it can also be detrimental by eliminating or dislocating jobs.

- **Computers and security:** Because internet-connected devices are becoming common components in the industry and in people's lives, such devices become more vulnerable to security attacks from individual hackers as well as organized cyberattacks. Cyberattacks can potentially lead to cyber-wars. Constantly improving the security of computing is one of the most significant world issues.

- **Computer industry career opportunities:** The industry employs over 10 percent of the world's workers. Some of the most in-demand jobs include research engineers, security experts, software engineers, and AI experts. Software engineers in software development jobs are in the highest demand.

John felt good about this list, since it provided him with a framework for thinking about how computers might fit into his college major and ultimately his career plans. At the highest level, he had moved his knowledge of computing from a user point of view to an appreciation of computing as an industry and as an enabler for all other industries and fields.

Having completed the MegaCepts process, John rated himself again on his knowledge of the topic:

- Education on the topic: 6
- Understanding of the topic: 6
- Confidence about the topic: 5
- Ability to provide leadership on the topic: 4
- Current satisfaction regarding the topic: 4
- Total score: 25 versus 12 at the beginning of the process

John more than doubled his initial rating with improvement in all areas. His improved education and understanding provided him with an organized, structured way to think about computer science to consider his college major decision more intelligently. He also built his personal "owned and understood" points that will help him further develop and continuously improve his understanding of computer science in the future.

"I liked the process of establishing the greatest thoughts relating to computer science," John told me, "since it made me think about it first, and then I augmented that thinking with other sources. I plan to use the process for any topic that I want to understand better, including all my college courses."

John used his MegaCepts list to make a significant decision and select his college major as he entered his sophomore year. He decided to pursue a double major that combines biology and computer science. That way, he could continue to pursue his strong interest in biology while also becoming proficient in computer science and be able to apply powerful technology to biological research. As he socialized this decision with his professors, family, and friends, he felt he had reached a conclusion that applies to everyone in today's world: "Regardless of one's educational, professional, or societal interests, gaining an appreciation and understanding of computer science is becoming an essential need."

Exercise

Before further illustrating the MegaCepts process in the next few chapters, I want to leave you with a short exercise.

In Chapters 5 and 6 you saw how two people applied the MegaCepts process to better think about topics that were important to them. It was easy and gratifying for them, as you can see by their outcomes. Why not pick an important topic in your life and try the MegaCepts process yourself?

You might first apply the process to a relatively easy personal topic, such as, "How can I clean my house effectively each week?" or "How can I be well organized for grocery shopping each week?" or "How can I streamline my morning routine, so my kids and I can get to school and work on time—and with less stress."

You might also apply the MegaCepts process to a more challenging personal topic, such as, "How can I be a better spouse?" or "How can I advance my career?"

After finishing this book, you may want to apply this process of identifying your greatest thoughts to an even more complex topic, such as, "What are my true political beliefs?" or "What can I do to improve the environment in a significant, lasting way?"

I strongly believe this experience will be interesting, rewarding, and fun for you. Try it and see if you like it, then let me know either way! Contact me at Dave@MegaThinkingBook.com.

Brief Thoughts about John's MegaCepts Process

About 66 percent of US high school graduates attend college. One of the most important decisions they make that can affect the rest of their lives is picking a college major. John's process of using his final MegaCepts list to make this decision means he has a better chance of having made the best decision for his college career and professional career.

As I explained in Chapter 1, I made a significant decision when I decided to study aeronautical engineering. Initially, I had considered studying architecture. However, my decision enabled me to progress from college into computer science in business and that, in turn, became the basis for my entire career in information technology. I might have been happy being an architect, but it never would have been like the experience and success I have had in the exploding field of computing.

"When all else fails, try thinking."

—UNKNOWN AUTHOR

Applying the MegaCepts Process to Improve Interpersonal Skills for Career Development

"They can do all because they think they can."

—VIRGIL

A nother way to apply the MegaCepts process is to pick a topic you want to study until you are an expert on it. Such topics could be important subjects in school, urgent family health matters, or a personal financial plan. This chapter provides an example of someone who wanted to learn more about an important career-development and leadership topic.

Neil is in his fifth year of work after graduating from college with an engineering degree, and he is a respected software developer with his current employer. His logical and mathematical intelligence is very strong. Each year, he receives excellent reviews from his manager. However, in his last review, he asked his manager why he hadn't received a promotion to become a manager of other software engineers. His manager responded that despite his very strong technical skills, his people management skills were not strong enough for promotion to manager.

The manager, who was an experienced, strong leader, explained to Neil that people skills—which he further defined as interpersonal skills—were extremely important. He said interpersonal intelligence was one of the eight types of intelligence defined by developmental psychologist Howard Gardner. Gardner originally developed his Theory of Multiple Intelligences in his groundbreaking 1983 book, *Frames of Mind: The Theory of Multiple Intelligences.*

Neil asked his manager how he might learn more about interpersonal skills. The manager immediately recommended his favorite book on that subject: Dale Carnegie's *How to Win Friends and Influence People.* He told Neil his first manager had recommended this book and that reading it had a significant and positive impact on both his career and his personal life. Neil immediately committed to buy, read, and study the book.

Once Neil got the book, he immediately felt a little intimidated, since it was written by a famous author and is the most successful self-help book of all time, having sold over thirty-five million copies. He initially scanned the book, and it looked very detailed and complex. So, he decided to apply the MegaCepts process to reading, studying, and thinking about the book. He felt the process could help simplify the complexity and allow him to think more clearly about the most important ideas regarding interpersonal skills and relationships.

Before reading and thinking about the book, Neil rated himself as follows on his understanding of interpersonal skills and relationships on a scale of one to ten:

- Education on the topic: 2
- Understanding of the topic: 3
- Confidence about the topic: 2
- Ability to provide leadership on the topic: 1
- Current satisfaction regarding the topic: 2
- Total score: 10

This low "going in" score—only ten points out of a possible fifty—further convinced Neil that he needed to study and improve his interpersonal intelligence and skills. His education, understanding, and confidence were all low, in large part because most of his formal education had been in highly technical engineering topics, not in topics related to people or management. He also had not taken time to read about interpersonal skills and relationships. Without either formal or personal education on this topic, it is hard to have understanding, and without understanding it's impossible to have confidence. Without these fundamentals, it is impossible to be a leader on the subject. So, Neil started with a low satisfaction level, but he was eager to improve that score by reading Dale Carnegie's book and applying the MegaCepts process.

At the beginning of his book, Carnegie recommends that to get the most out of it, the reader should adhere to a list of nine practices, including reading each chapter twice, reviewing the book each month, and underlining each important idea. Neil made a commitment to follow through with each of these recommendations. These instructions caused Neil to commit, focus, think, and understand the book's ideas much better than he would have normally done while reading a book.

After reading the book and keeping notes, Neil began the MegaCepts process.

Step 1: Neil's Initial Ideas

Neil reviewed all the notes he took while reading the book and really thought about what they meant and how important they were. He then wrote down his best thoughts on the topic of interpersonal skills and relationships. He did this in a few steps, first getting thoughts down quickly and then coming back and revising them a few more times over the next few days.

This is an essential step, since it is the beginning of your thinking on the topic. By taking this step, you are forcing yourself to think independently. Neil tried to express his initial ideas as completely and concisely as possible. He also tried to state them in terms that were the most meaningful and understandable to him rather than just repeating the same words from the book.

After reading the book, his initial ideas were:

- **Prioritizing people and relationships:** Genuinely make other people a personal priority.

- **Remembering the critical importance of listening:** Listen, listen, listen. Ask, ask, ask. Let the other person do most of the talking. It is important to both understand the other person's point of view and let them know you value their thoughts.

- **Reaching mutual conclusions and agreements:** Try to make the conclusion(s) in a discussion be the other person's idea(s). Then compliment and praise them for that. At the end of the discussion, try to make all conclusions and decisions mutual.

Neil knew the book contained many other ideas, but he felt these were the most important ones for his situation. His goals during the next steps of the process were to reinforce these points and add other new ideas. This kind of initial list of ideas on a complex topic is typical when a person is first studying and thinking about that topic.

Step 2: Neil's Socialized Ideas

Neil decided to socialize the topic of interpersonal skills and relationships with three people. One was his manager—the one who had guided him to read Dale Carnegie's book in the first place. The two others were friends whose careers had progressed into management. In all three cases, he asked for their initial thoughts on this topic without guiding them. After that, he asked each of them a series of specific questions that related to his initial ideas from reading the book. In all three cases, he found a strong alignment with his initial ideas.

One point that all three professionals focused on was the importance of genuinely respecting people for their skills, thoughts, and feelings. They all expressed that if someone perceived that your thoughts and feelings were not genuine, then all other interpersonal relationship skills would fail. This was a key take-away in his discussions with all three professionals.

Another consensus idea was the importance of positively questioning and listening to people. This shows the person you genuinely care about them and are open to their ideas. A person who does not listen well will be perceived as a person who doesn't care.

One of Neil's friends who, as vice president of his company, had achieved the highest level of business success among the three people, emphasized the importance of developing strong leadership skills. This not only strongly compliments your other interpersonal skills, but it also influences others to respect and follow you.

Neil concluded that all three of these points would be important to emphasize in his final thoughts.

Step 3: Neil's Research Ideas

Next, Neil searched the topic on the internet, using search terms such as "key principles of how to win friends and influence people" and "key principles of interpersonal intelligence and relationships." One article he found particularly valuable was, "How to Win Friends and Influence People: The Principles" by Samuel Thomas Davies.

Through his research, Neil identified twelve different principles in the areas of working effectively with people, genuinely getting people to like and respect you, and leading people. He studied these and compared them with his initial list of ideas, and about half were the same or similar. He finally selected five new ideas to integrate with his initial list. He was also looking for more thoughts on how to achieve the desired results of improving his interpersonal skills and relationships.

Two of these new ideas amplified the importance of some of his initial ideas. For example, he found that his point regarding "the importance of people and relationships" needed to be emphasized, so he decided to stress the idea of genuinely committing to making people important to you and making people feel important.

Step 4: Neil's MegaCepts List

Neil integrated his initial ideas with those from his socialized and research steps to produce the following list of his greatest thoughts.

Demonstrate that people are important: Genuinely commit to always making people important and a priority to you in all dealings with them, whether that is one-on-one or in groups. Make people the most important thing in your life and in the world. Golden Rule: "Do unto others as you as would have them do unto you."

- **Lead people effectively:** Lead people by motivating them to follow you on a given thought, topic, or plan. People like to follow strong, positive leaders. People leaders are positive, participative, and charismatic. Lead sensitively but confidently, not insensitively and arrogantly. Be humble and flexible but not so flexible that you undermine your ultimate position(s). "Be flexible but not limp."

- **Build relationships with people:** Work hard to get people to like and respect you. Be genuinely interested in other people. Respect them, listen to them, and appreciate them.

- **Have discussions with people:** Try to take the "high road" on every point of the discussion. Ask what is in the best interest of the team, family, or organization rather than the individuals involved. Show respect for the other person's point of view. Listen, ask questions, and let the other person do most of the talking.

- **Discuss topics in a focused way:** Focus on the key facts and principles of a topic, not on your opinions and prejudices or the other person's opinions and prejudices. Focus on the objective realities of the discussion and seek the best "mutual truth" on a topic.

- **Make mutual conclusions:** Apply the above five approaches to give the other person credit for the final conclusion(s) in a discussion. Then thank them for that. At the end of the discussion, try to make all conclusions and decisions mutual.

These are the six MegaCepts that Neil will use to significantly improve his interpersonal intelligence and people skills. He felt good that this list was intelligently structured and that it emphasized what the book, his research, and his colleagues had indicated as the most important points. He also felt this list offered a great way to further socialize this topic with others, and he planned to do that actively.

After establishing the above list, Neil rated himself again on this subject:

- Education on the topic: 6
- Understanding of the topic: 6
- Confidence about the topic: 4
- Ability to provide leadership on the topic: 4
- Current satisfaction regarding the topic: 5
- Total score: 25 versus 10 at the beginning of the process

As Neil's self-rating attests, his ability to think about and understand how to improve his interpersonal relationships has dramatically improved using a simple process that took only about ten hours after reading the book. His education and understanding scores increased dramatically. His confidence and leadership scores did not increase as rapidly, but these will increase more as he has more time to execute on his new understanding. His overall satisfaction score should also increase over time as well. All of this is an incredibly high return on his time investment.

Neil will immediately use his new understanding to try to expand his career opportunities into valuable management and leadership roles. Every chance he gets, he will socialize the topic with others, using his MegaCepts list as the outline or framework for the discussion. Using these as inputs, he will continuously refine his greatest thoughts. This will also make him more articulate on the topic, and he will rapidly become a knowledgeable expert on the topic in his own eyes and other's eyes. This will also reinforce his confidence that he can apply the knowledge now.

"Before I read Dale Carnegie's book on interpersonal relationships," he told me, "I was intimidated by the thought of getting better in this area. Even as I read the book, I felt a bit overwhelmed by the amount of information I was trying to comprehend and think about. But by applying the MegaCepts process to both the book and my subsequent research I was able to understand the most important concepts about interpersonal skills. I now feel confident in applying them to advance my career. A major side benefit is that this skill has provided significant benefits in my personal life with my family and friends!"

Brief Thoughts about Interpersonal Skills

As explained in this chapter, developmental psychologist Howard Gardner defined eight types of intelligence in his book, *Frames of Mind: The Theory of Multiple Intelligences*. One of the eight is logical-mathematical intelligence, which many people believe is the most important. But as you proceed through your life a good case can be made that the most important intelligence is interpersonal skills. It is worth reading this book or simply searching for a summary on the internet to understand all eight forms of intelligence.

I had a career challenge during my first year after joining IBM. During that first year I spent about eight months in various computer science training courses. My engineering background allowed me to excel in these courses. At the end of the first year, I started attending marketing and sales training courses that involved making presentations and dealing with people. I didn't do as well in those courses, so my manager enrolled me in an eleven-week Dale Carnegie course and asked me to read Carnegie's book, *How to Win Friends and Influence People*. That was an incredibly significant experience that led to developing my interpersonal skills to a level that benefited my entire career and life.

"Few minds wear out, most rust out."

—CHRISTIAN BOYCE

CHAPTER 8

Applying the MegaCepts Process to Understand Artificial Intelligence

"Thoughts rule the world."

—RALPH WALDO EMERSON

Artificial intelligence (AI) is one of the most important technologies that has already affected the world in many ways, and those effects will increase dramatically in the coming decades as AI is developed with even more powerful capabilities. AI leverages computers and machines to mimic the problem-solving and decision-making capabilities of the human mind. Along with Apple's Siri, mentioned in Chapter 6, Alexa from Amazon is another virtual assistant that responds to user commands and questions.

Todd was in the process of a career change from consumer marketing to computer marketing. Since AI is one of the most significant advances in computing, he was particularly interested in getting involved with this technology in this career change. He also chose AI because it is still new enough to most people in the computer industry that he would not start far behind the rest of the industry in understanding and implementing it.

Todd had begun to study the field but was interested in learning and understanding more so that when he was interviewed for potential AI-related jobs, he would come across as knowledgeable. He decided to use the MegaCepts process to study and learn more about AI. The specific topic he wanted to study was, in his own words, "understanding an overview of AI—what it is, how it works, and how it is used and applied."

The first source he studied was an IBM education course on AI titled, "What is Artificial Intelligence (AI)?" Todd knows that IBM has been one of the most significant contributors to the computing and information age and is one of the leaders in AI via the company's Watson initiative. IBM provides excellent education and training on all computer-related subjects. The IBM AI education program also contains many other references on AI from sources such as Alan Turing's seminal paper, "Computing Machinery and Intelligence," Stuart Russell and Peter Norvig's *Artificial Intelligence: A Modern Approach*, and John McCarthy's "What is Artificial Intelligence: The Ethics of AI."

Before taking the IBM course, Todd rated himself regarding the AI topic on a scale of one to ten:

- Education on the topic: 2
- Understanding of the topic: 2
- Confidence about the topic: 2
- Ability to provide leadership on the topic: 1
- Current satisfaction regarding the topic: 1
- Total score: 8

Todd's low scores on education, understanding, and confidence are all linked to the fact that his career had been in consumer marketing, not computer marketing. He had not received any formal computer or AI training and had no relevant job experience. Without these qualifications, he scored himself even lower on leadership and satisfaction. Given his strong desire to change his career focus, he was highly motivated to do whatever he needed to become knowledgeable about AI. This is the proper mindset to have when you are studying a new, complex subject.

Step 1: Todd's Initial Ideas

Todd's initial list of ideas on AI was relatively short. The IBM course was extensive and complex, and the multiple additional research sources referenced in the course made learning about this subject even more intimidating. So, he only listed those ideas in which he felt confident about being accurate. He knew he would be going back to review more about AI from the course and the other references again. He also knew a step in the MegaCepts process was to conduct additional research.

Here are Todd's initial ideas:

- **AI defined:** AI is generally defined as computer-based intelligence with several sub-definitions:

  - Human approaches: Systems that think like humans and systems that act like humans.

  - Ideal approaches: Systems that think rationally and systems that act rationally.

  - More simply, AI is a field that combines computer science and robust datasets to enable problem solving.

- **AI types:** Two major types of AI:

  - Weak AI or narrow AI: Examples include applications such as IBM's Watson, digital assistants such as Apple's Siri, and most importantly today, generative AI such as OpenAI's ChatGPT.

  - Strong AI or artificial general intelligence (AGI) or artificial super intelligence (ASI): This is where a computer or machine would have intelligence equal to, or even superior to, humans. A fictional example of this would be HAL 9000, the rogue computer assistant in the movie *2001: A Space Odyssey*.

- **AI applications:** Major application categories of AI in today's world include the following, which are all weak/narrow, machine-learning based:

  - Web search engines, gaming, expert systems, handwriting recognition, intelligent robots, speech recognition, customer service, computer vision, recommendation engines, and automated stock trading.

Since Todd was just beginning to study AI, this was a good initial list of ideas. He knew the IBM course presented many more important points, but by focusing on these three initial, most important points, he had already established a valuable framework to add additional points. Think of it this way: Before taking the IBM course and establishing the above three ideas, he would not have been able to have an intelligent conversation with anyone about his AI career aspirations. By taking the course and establishing these three points, he was already able to have that type of conversation. For example, Todd has a friend who has worked in the computer business his entire career, though not focused on AI. Todd could now tell the friend about his desire to get into the computer/AI industry. He could then recite his animated version of the above three points. The friend would probably be interested to hear Todd's articulation of AI's definition, types, and applications and would probably volunteer to help Todd in his career search.

One of the three most powerful results of applying organized and structured thinking on a complex subject such as AI is that it enables you to be perceived as knowledgeable with minimal education and experience.

Step 2: Todd's Socialized Ideas

When Todd attended college he majored in communications, not engineering or computer sciences, which led to his career in consumer sales and marketing. Two of his best friends in college majored in electrical engineering and computer sciences, and after college they both developed their careers in the computer industry, so Todd sought out both friends to get their input on the subject of AI.

The engineer had focused his career on software development. Recently, he started to work in AI-related software, with an emphasis on voice recognition and response. His key input to Todd was to focus on the most important applications of AI that exist today and will continue to improve in the future. His specific example was how Siri revolutionized how people use their smartphones to ask questions and receive answers, including how to drive from point A to point B. He feels it will be a long time before AI technology will advance to the point that it could replicate the human brain and not only think but also "feel."

The computer science major had focused his career on computer marketing. He had been exposed to AI as it was being applied to computer security. This exposure led him to believe that AI presents major industry and societal challenges in the areas of ethics, privacy, and the impact on jobs.

Todd internalized these inputs and committed to reflect them in his final thoughts on AI.

Step 3: Todd's Research Ideas

Todd's research focus was not only to find new, more important AI ideas but also to learn how to achieve these ideas. Let's call those the "what's" and "how's" of AI. He searched the topic on the internet using phrases like, "What is AI, and how does it work?" "AI explained," and "Applications of AI." Given the importance of AI, he found hundreds of references to articles, research, and books on the subject. He scanned a number of them to find the ones that added the most additional understanding to the IBM AI education course. He found relevant articles and research with topics such as AI overview, types, and machine learning; AI definition and examples; and AI explained.

Todd took notes on each of these and selected the most important additional ideas to integrate with his original IBM training-based idea list. Some of those included the following discoveries. First, he found some easier-to-understand explanations of AI types. The IBM course was quite technology focused, and his new research made this topic more understandable to him. He defined these as the most important sub-definitions of AI. Second, he found some valuable research on the levels of AI, which was again presented in a way that made it easier for him to understand and apply than what the IBM course had provided.

Another research topic he found fascinating but, in some ways, potentially conflicting with the IBM course was AI ethics and AI and society. The IBM course tended to side on the positive side of both topics. The research sources tended to take a more conservative and at times almost negative view. Todd decided that his final MegaCepts list would present a balance of the positive and negative views on these topics.

Step 4: Todd's MegaCepts List

AI is extensive in scope and very complex, and there are many such subjects in life. The MegaCepts for topics like this are necessarily also more complex. As Todd's MegaCepts list illustrates, it is important to define each of the high-level greatest thoughts as simply and clearly as possible, and then add more detail as necessary to explain what it is and how to achieve it in sufficient depth to assure understanding.

Todd's final MegaCepts list was quite detailed; the highlights follow:

- **The best general AI definition:** AI leverages computers and machines to mimic the problem-solving and decision-making capabilities of the human mind. It is a constellation of many different technologies working together to sense, comprehend, act, and learn with human levels of intelligence such as perceiving, learning, reasoning, and problem solving.

- According to the "father of artificial intelligence," John McCarthy, AI is "the science and engineering of making intelligent machines, especially intelligent computer programs."

- The goal of AI is to create systems that can perform tasks that would otherwise require human intelligence. AI is the ability of a machine to perform cognitive functions as humans do.

- Multiple science and technology-based disciplines contribute to AI, including computer science, biology, psychology, linguistics, mathematics, and engineering.

- **AI has four important sub-definitions:**

  - Human approaches: Systems that think like humans and act like humans.

  - Ideal approaches: Systems that think rationally and act rationally.

  - Sub-fields of AI include machine learning and deep learning. Machine learning is comprised of AI algorithms that seek to create expert systems that make predictions or classifications based on input data. Deep learning is a sub-field of machine learning. It uses neural networks with three or more layers to further automate the learning process.

  - The underlying technology that enables deep learning is neural networks, which simulate how the human brain works by taking in multiple input layers and analyzing them with multiple "hidden layers" that then feed into multiple output layers. A neural network is an inter-connected group of nodes, akin to the vast network of neurons in the human brain.

- **AI has two major "levels" of capabilities:**

  - Weak or narrow AI: This is the predominant form of AI today and is made up of intelligent systems that know how to conduct specific tasks without having been explicitly programmed to do so. These systems simulate a human's knowledge and cognitive ability within specific parameters. Examples include Apple's Siri and Amazon's Alexa.

  - Strong AI or artificial general intelligence (AGI) or artificial super intelligence (ASI): This form of AI is called "strong" because it will be stronger than human intelligence, and it is called "general" because it will be applied to all problems. A fictional example of this would be HAL 9000, the rogue computer assistant in *2001: A Space Odyssey*. Today, AI remains an extension of human capabilities, not a replacement. But technologists believe that will change in the future.

- **The major application categories of AI include:**

  - Speech recognition, customer service, computer vision (one of the technologies that makes self-driving cars feasible), recommendation engines, and automated stock trading.

- **The most important historical events and future predictions in AI are:**

  - History: Todd listed multiple historical milestones in the development of artificial intelligence, adding: The first two decades of the twenty-first century have seen an acceleration of machine learning-based, weak or narrow AI applications.

  - Future: The next two decades will see a proliferation of even more sophisticated machine-learning AI applications, such as driverless vehicles and more advanced robotics.

- **Why the subject of AI ethics is important:** There is plenty of cause for concern when facing the reality of machines that can literally think for themselves. Think of HAL 9000 making decisions independent of humans in *2001: A Space Odyssey*!

  - AI ethics is a set of guidelines that advise on the design and outcomes of AI, including respect for people, beneficence, justice, and the reduction of bias.

  - Given the importance of AI ethics, several dedicated organizations have been established to focus on this issue.

- **AI's impact on society:** There are multiple concerns about how AI might impact our society, including technological singularity (the fear that AI will eventually surpass human intelligence), a negative impact on jobs, privacy, and cybersecurity.

Todd will utilize these seven most important MegaCepts to demonstrate his knowledge of AI in his career change. Note that several of them are not simple statements that can be easily memorized like "thou shalt not kill." However, these greatest thoughts are organized "containers" that capture a specific category of thoughts, which Todd can easily return to and embellish. Moving forward, he will further support his seven MegaCepts as he sees fit by accessing his more detailed notes. He will also continuously improve each of them by socializing them with anyone who is also interested in AI.

By thinking about and establishing these greatest thoughts in a structured and organized way, Todd is now able to discuss this topic with virtually anyone and be perceived as intelligent, knowledgeable, and articulate. The friend whom Todd spoke with about his initial ideas on AI was surprised by his high-level understanding of AI after he took the IBM course. But once Todd completed the MegaCepts process, his friend was incredibly impressed with Todd's ability to intelligently discuss AI.

Todd rated himself again as follows:

- Education on the topic: 6
- Understanding of the topic: 6
- Confidence about the topic: 5
- Ability to provide leadership on the topic: 4

- Current satisfaction regarding the topic: 6
- Total score: 27 versus 8 at the beginning of the process

Todd's dramatic improvement in these scores is understandable. He is bright and strongly motivated to make this major career change. His educational sources were high quality, and he studied them diligently—dramatically improving his understanding and confidence. I think the only reason his leadership score is not higher is that he has not yet had time to actually interact with others on this topic, including AI-literate people. After he has done so, I believe his self-assessed leadership score will naturally rise.

The improvements in his score are due to his focus on the greatest thoughts on AI, which helped him avoid getting lost in the incredible details and complexity of the topic. He established his own context and framework for thinking about AI. This form of simple but powerful, structured thinking is the best way to understand any topic.

"AI is an extremely important and complex subject," Todd told me after completing the process. "I was initially intimidated and overwhelmed by the task of becoming knowledgeable enough to be able to pursue a career in the field. Taking a good AI course from IBM was beneficial, but it was very extensive and complex, and I found myself getting lost in the complexity and detail. Applying the MegaCepts process forced me to identify the most important points about AI and capture them in a logical, structured, and understandable way."

Exercise

In the next two chapters, I will show how even someone who is an expert in their field can use the MegaCepts process to better understand their topic. But first I want to leave you with a short exercise relating to Chapters 7 and 8. You have just read about how two people, Neil and Todd, applied the MegaCepts process to fairly complex topics that they wanted to study in depth, so they would become knowledgeable about them.

Neil's focus on interpersonal relationships stemmed from his desire to become a manager, and Todd's focus was also career oriented. He wanted to change his industry focus from the consumer field into the computer field, with a particular focus on AI. Both accomplished their objectives, and both are now pursuing their new, successful careers.

Now, I would like you to pick a complex subject about which you would like to become more knowledgeable. Choose a topic that is particularly interesting to you and potentially valuable in your personal or professional life. Ideally, you would find it satisfying to gain additional knowledge by using the MegaCepts process to learn more about this topic. The list of available topics is large, so pick one that is especially important to you right now, apply the MegaCepts process to it, and just like Neil and Todd did, see what your greatest thoughts look like at the end of the process.

If your experience is anything like that of Neil and Todd's, you will be pleased with the result. Let me know how it goes by sending an email to me at Dave@MegaThinkingBook.com.

Brief Thoughts about Todd's MegaCepts Process and AI

According to many experts, AI will have the most significant impact on information technology and its application of any technology in the history of the information age. Todd's MegaCepts process clearly emphasized and illustrated that AI is very important and complex. This chapter provides you with an excellent framework to pursue additional study and thinking about this incredibly important topic.

I am on the Board of Trustees of the Computer History Museum (CHM), which is the leading worldwide institution focused on the history of and future for all things related to information technology. The CHM leadership has made AI their highest priority to provide thought leadership on:

- The technology itself, including its many types such as generative AI and machine learning.

- Its many applications, such as query systems and self-driving vehicles.

- The impacts it will have on entire industries, such as healthcare and education.

- The potential positive and negative impacts on society, such as positive productivity improvements and negative impacts such as job losses.

If you plan to study and think more about AI, one source of information would be the CHM website, www.ComputerHistory.org.

"If there was one life skill everyone on the planet needed it was the ability to think with critical objectivity."

—HENRY DAVID THOREAU

CHAPTER 9

Applying the MegaCepts Process to Become a Great Leader

"Thinking is easy, acting is difficult, and to put one's thoughts into action is the most difficult thing in the world."

—JOHANN WOLFGANG VON GOETHE

Leadership is one of the most important human skills, impacting every aspect of society, including government, the military, business, nonprofits, education, healthcare, religion, the arts, and sports. Good leadership is the most important ingredient for success in all these areas, and bad leadership is the most important reason for failure. Inspired leadership can transform the world, such as Martin Luther King Jr.'s stirring leadership in the civil rights movement, while evil leadership can cause catastrophic harm, such as Hitler's leadership of Germany into the second World War, which produced the Holocaust, among many other atrocities.

Some of the most relevant synonyms for leadership include coaching, captainship, guidance, overseeing, and tutelage. People often equate leadership and management, but they are quite different. The most powerful leaders are not always the best managers and vice versa. There is an often-stated contrast between the two: "Leaders do the right things, and managers do things right." Thinking is important on any topic, including becoming an effective leader.

Ray is a positive, intelligent thinker, and he is also an experienced and acknowledged business, investment, and educational leader. He has coached a number of business executives, nonprofit institutional managers, and others on how to be a better leader. One of the key principles in his personal and professional life is that you should never stop your learning process on important topics, even if you think you are already an expert.

He decided to apply the MegaCepts process to further his learning and understanding of the key principles of effective leadership. He started with his own extensive knowledge and expertise and then enhanced that even further with the MegaCepts process. His goal was to understand new ideas about leadership based on the most current thinking.

Ray was particularly interested in understanding how the current business and societal environment has influenced important new leadership approaches. He wanted to know how the leadership of people from the Traditionalist Generation (also known as the Silent Generation or Greatest Generation) and Baby Boomer Generation (pre-1945 to 1964) had progressed to the leadership seen in the Generation X and Y period (1965 to 1995) and how it is now being practiced in the Generation Z period (1996 to about 2015).

As he started the process, Ray rated himself on a scale of one to ten this way:

- Education on the topic: 6
- Understanding of the topic: 7
- Confidence about the topic: 7
- Ability to provide leadership on the topic: 8
- Current satisfaction regarding the topic: 7
- Total score: 35

Ray's education in leadership was mostly the on-the-job training. He educated himself by learning to lead with little or no formal education. His understanding and confidence are high due to his more than forty years of actual leadership. His ability to lead on this topic is even higher, since he has spent decades coaching others on this topic. Although his current satisfaction level on the topic is high, he has made it a point throughout his entire career and life always to improve.

Step 1: Ray's Initial Ideas

Ray wrote down his best initial thoughts on the leadership topic. These ideas are what he has used personally for decades and what he has been training other leaders to use as well. Since he is a strong believer in focus, he narrowed his initial leadership ideas down to the four most important ones:

- **Interpersonal skills:** Develop and employ strong interpersonal skills with people; leadership is about people. Interpersonal and communication skills are essential to any leader. Without being able to communicate your vision to others, leadership will be challenging. Key interpersonal skills and styles include being genuine, respecting others, being a good listener, asking lots of questions, making the other person feel important, and giving honest and sincere appreciation.

- **Participative leadership:** Practice and promote this leadership style in which all members of the organization work together to make decisions. Participative leadership is democratic leadership, as everyone is encouraged to participate. Key steps in participative leadership include discussing everything as a group, providing relevant information to everyone, encouraging the sharing of ideas, processing and summarizing ideas and information, making a group decision by gaining consensus agreement, and implementing the decision with unanimity as a team.

- **Team building:** Focus on team togetherness and team execution. Strong leaders know they will not be successful without optimum team support. You must know how to encourage teamwork and collaboration, inspire team members to contribute their best work, and motivate colleagues to accomplish difficult and challenging tasks. Key steps in building an effective team include establishing your strong leadership by getting people to respect your judgment and your professional and personal treatment of them as individuals and as a total team, establishing personal relationships with each of your team members, encouraging the building of relationships among the members of the team, and fostering teamwork by encouraging each team member to share information, communicate with everyone, and "do unto others as they would have others do unto them." Set clear objectives and ground rules for the team. Measure the achievement of these objectives and the adherence to the ground rules as individuals and as a team.

- **Lead by example:** Good leaders demonstrate how to behave, perform tasks, and do their work. A good leader provides a model for excellent behavior to lead and motivate the team. The team should see that you are confident and dedicated. This will cause them to want to align their behavior with their leader's behavior. Everything the leader does will be reflected in the actions of the team. "Lead from the front" with confidence and decisiveness.

Ray's initial ideas on leadership were powerful and proven, so he was confident they would be on his final MegaCepts list. But he also knew from experience that he would probably expand his final list via further research and organized thinking.

Step 2: Ray's Socialized Ideas

Having coached a number of people over the last few decades on how to be a better leader, Ray decided to contact two of the younger people he originally coached to discuss how their approaches to leadership had evolved since Ray had first coached them. He was particularly interested in seeing how these approaches had changed from his original coaching points, and he wanted to specifically understand how they had adapted their leadership approaches to the younger generations.

Ray left these discussions with a better understanding that the younger generations want to be led by someone with strong beliefs and principles in the areas they think are most important in society today, such as the environment, minority rights, and free speech. Ray understood that it was key to acknowledge the importance of these areas but not necessarily to agree with everyone on them. Another point he gleaned from the discussions was the value of being a strong, positive leader. Society today is more complex than in the past, and the younger generations feel more pressure and anxiety over some societal and personal issues. Consequently, being positive, personable, and charismatic is much more important for a leader now than it was in the past when many leaders were strong but also cold and dictatorial.

Step 3: Ray's Research Ideas

In developing his own leadership skills and coaching others on how to be a better leader, Ray has read many books on leadership. So, rather than focus on book research, he decided to conduct an internet search for the latest articles focused on the key principles of effective, participative leadership. He looked at about twenty articles and research papers and identified five articles as the most relevant to potentially expand and strengthen his own leadership ideas.

Those five articles contained seventy-two principles in total, with fifty-three of them being unique. Ray reviewed them all and decided that the following five were the most relevant new leadership ideas from this research and should be integrated with his initial idea list: inspirational leadership, interpersonal skills, participatory leadership, team building, and decisiveness. In selecting these five, he chose ideas that added the newest thinking about the topic, such as a focus on strong personal character traits. Other ideas were complementary and reinforcing.

He liked that a number of articles emphasized developing and displaying your own strong, personal qualities, since he knew this was more important today than it was in the past.

Ray also liked the emphasis on leaders providing inspiration by being charismatic. This was clearly not a new idea for him regarding good leadership, but he saw it as an even more important point in today's world. He thought about people like basketball coach John Wooden, the "Wizard of Westwood," who guided UCLA to a record number of NCAA basketball championships and achieved it with not only detailed leadership skills but also with genuine charisma—even his competitors loved him for that!

Ray also liked the emphasis on leadership decisiveness, which has always been important in leadership. But again, in today's world, that quality is even more valuable due to the rapidity of change. Leadership decisiveness is connected to another idea from his research, which is to lead *through* change since no topic, process, or activity is static.

Step 4: Ray's MegaCepts List

Ray reflected on his initial ideas, socialized ideas, and research ideas and rank ordered them from most important to least important. He put a special emphasis on the socialized ideas from his previous coaching clients, since he respected them and their views of what is important to younger generations.

Ray's resulting greatest thoughts for how to become a better leader are listed below. "What to focus on" is shown in bold, and "how to achieve the focus" follows.

- **Personal character traits:** Develop and visibly show your own high-quality personal character traits. These traits will cause the people you are leading to respect you and follow you. These traits include genuineness, empathy, patience, authenticity, integrity, ethics, sensitivity to and acceptance of key societal issues, and maturity.

- **Inspirational leadership:** Provide inspiration to those you are leading. This should be achieved by speaking in a charismatic way. Have a strong, positive, and passionate vision for, and purpose in, what you are leading toward. Show curiosity and creativity toward what others think about the activity that you are leading in. Lead by example; "lead from the front."

- **Interpersonal skills:** Strong interpersonal skills are critical to leading people. Interpersonal intelligence is one of the nine recognized types of intelligence. It is the ability to understand and interact effectively with others. It involves effective verbal and nonverbal communication, the ability to note distinctions among other people, sensitivity to the moods and temperaments of others, and the ability to entertain multiple perspectives. Leadership is about people, and interpersonal skills are essential to leading people.

- **Participative leadership:** Properly practiced, participative leadership can be the most powerful way to lead, since all members of the organization are encouraged to work together to make decisions. Everyone in the group is provided with the same essential information, and everything is discussed openly as a group. Decisions are made by consensus within the group, not by leadership dictates.

- **Team building:** A focus on team building is essential if you want to be a strong leader. Strong leaders know this and always focus on it as a fundamental requirement for success. The first step in building a team is to assert your own strong leadership on the importance of building teams. Your team needs to believe that you believe in this. The second step is to recruit or assign the strongest individual members of the team where their collective talents and achievements will far exceed any one individual's talents and achievements. The team then needs to perform in a participative and mutually reinforcing way. The team spirit, led by the leader, needs to be "All for one and one for all."

- **Decisiveness:** Be decisive and assertive once a topic, process, or activity has been openly and thoroughly discussed. People respect ultimately decisive leaders. Decisiveness shows confidence, commitment, courage, resourcefulness, resilience, influence, focus, innovation, and willingness to change (if required). Avoid "paralysis by analysis" and "making a decision not to decide" (aka "kicking the can down the road").

Ray rated himself again on the topic of leadership as follows:

- Education on the topic: 8
- Understanding of the topic: 8
- Confidence about the topic: 9
- Ability to provide leadership on the topic: 8
- Current satisfaction regarding the topic: 9
- Total score: 42 versus 35 before he began the process

Ray was a bit surprised at how much his rating improved, and I think this was because, through the socializing and research steps, he further recognized the importance of strong personal character traits, decisiveness, and charismatic, inspirational leadership. He clearly understood that these were all related to the different mindsets of the younger generations.

Ray found that the MegaCepts process forced him to think about and understand leadership in an even more structured and organized way than he had used in the past. That made both his original and new ideas more understandable to him and the people he coaches.

"In the beginning, I was a bit skeptical that I would gain any significant knowledge about leadership by applying the MegaCepts process," he told me. "But the combination of learning some new, important ideas and the structured approach to thinking about, understanding, and communicating about leadership created a very positive and valuable result."

Brief Thoughts about Ray's MegaCepts Process and Leadership

As mentioned at the beginning of this chapter, many people equate management and leadership, but they are quite different. Ray's process and final greatest thoughts list fully illustrates this difference. Management requires the methodical execution of the rules and techniques you have been taught and stored in your memory. Leadership requires continuous thinking about what to do and how to do it.

This book's title clearly states this important linkage between leadership and thinking: *Mega Thinking: A Simple, Powerful Process to Think Smarter and Make Better Leadership Decisions*. My focus now is on making this book on thinking available to as many readers and leaders as possible. Once that is accomplished my next goal will be to write another book, which might be titled *The MegaCepts of Leadership Decision-Making*.

"Five percent of the people think; ten percent of the people think they think, and the other eighty-five percent would rather die than think."

—THOMAS EDISON

CHAPTER 10

Applying the MegaCepts Process to Reduce Medical Errors

"The important thing in science is not so much to obtain new facts as to discover new ways to think about them."

—WILLIAM BRAGG

One of the most important areas in society is healthcare. It is an enormous industry that exceeded 11.2 trillion dollars in 2021, according to Becker's Hospital Review. Healthcare quality and cost impact every one of the over eight billion people in the world, and one of the most significant issues in healthcare is the cost and suffering caused by medical errors. Such errors are the third most significant cause of death in the United States behind heart disease and cancer. Worldwide, medical errors cause over ten million deaths per year and cause over 140 million people per year to suffer serious medical harm.

Mary is a highly regarded surgeon who is also a professor at a well-known medical school. She is active in the healthcare industry promoting much-needed improvements, including reducing medical errors, so she is already an expert in this field. She realized the root causes of medical errors and the solutions to reduce these errors are dynamic due to the constantly changing injury, disease, and treatment environment.

The COVID-19 pandemic, which impacted the entire world, is a monumental example. At its onset in 2019, it was a new disease that dictated completely different treatment. Due to this upheaval, millions of medical errors occurred during the pandemic, and they were due to both "old" reasons and a completely new set of reasons. So, Mary decided to apply the MegaCepts process to the following topic: "What are the major causes of medical errors in the United States, and how can they be dramatically reduced?"

She had two primary goals. First, she wanted to use the MegaCepts process to break down this complex subject into ideas that would be easier to think about, easier to understand, and easier to communicate with patients, providers, and professionals. Second, she wanted to use the process to identify the newest ideas about the root causes of medical errors and associated solutions, including those that have been created by the extraordinary pandemic experience.

Mary is a strong advocate that learning in the medical field, as in life, is the work of a lifetime. She also knew that despite having been focused on reducing medical errors for decades—as a surgeon, as a member of her hospital staff, as a professor in medical school, and as a member of the healthcare industry—she had never formally written down, in rank order, the most important causes of today's medical errors. In that spirit, she applied the MegaCepts process to this topic.

On a scale of one to ten, Mary's self-rating at the start of the process was as follows:

- Education on the topic: 7
- Understanding of the topic: 7
- Confidence about the topic: 7
- Ability to provide leadership on the topic: 8
- Current satisfaction regarding the topic: 6
- Total score: 35

Given her background and experience, Mary's high scores in education, understanding, and confidence were understandable, and those qualities also drove her high leadership score. Her current satisfaction was lower, probably due to her ongoing belief that the subject is constantly changing, and the only way to be completely satisfied is to constantly repeat the education, understanding, and confidence cycle, which was exactly why she was motivated to apply the MegaCepts process. Despite her high score, she had the objectivity and drive to improve even further by thinking and understanding more about this important topic.

Step 1: Mary's Initial Ideas

Mary began the process by writing down her best thoughts on the topic. She had used these ideas personally and in training for decades. Since she is a strong believer in focus, she narrowed her initial list of ideas down to what she believed to be the four most important causes of medical errors:

- **Inadequate checklists:** Lack of rigorous, accurate, and complete use of medical procedure checklists directly at the point of patient care and based upon evidence-based medicine. Need to continuously update these checklists and make them available to the medical professional at the point of patient care.

- **Inadequate information flow:** Absence of a standard process of communicating information among the multiple medical professionals who take care of a patient. Need to provide a checklist of evidence-based steps that are objective, containing data points that all the medical professionals involved with a patient can access in real time during the entire caregiving process.

- **Poor human judgment:** Medical providers have variable levels of experience, knowledge, skill, and process understanding. Need to provide information technology-based systems that provide medical professionals with accurate, current training and process understanding.

- **Inadequate policies:** Staff is often unaware of hospital policies or a delayed policy to meet new and current practices. Need to include policies as part of an IT-based system to inform medical professionals about the latest policies related to the current treatment situation.

Step 2: Mary's Socialized Ideas

Given her extensive background, Mary interacts with a large group of medical professionals with a wide range of ages. She decided to discuss medical errors with two of the younger associates, both in their late thirties. Her goal was to get input from younger people with potentially fresh, new ideas on the subject of medical errors.

Both these younger medical professionals had one essential belief about medical errors: the most important way to reduce errors is to employ advanced IT software and systems that would improve the doctors', nurses', and physician associates' utilization of evidence-based best practices for all patient care processes. They believed the healthcare industry, both at the level of the individual professional as well as at the provider institutional level, has been reluctant to do that in the past.

One of Mary's associates expressed the opinion that some of this reluctance has been psychological, with professionals believing they were already experts and didn't need more technology to do their jobs better. Mary reflected that this was especially true for some of the more established professionals. In contrast, the younger generation was already starting to change this attitude, because they have grown up with IT as an integral part of their lives. Mary left these discussions with a much stronger belief in the importance of applying technology to the issue of medical errors.

Step 3: Mary's Research Ideas

From a search of the most recent and pertinent research, Mary found several articles to be the most valuable. These articles addressed the common root causes of medical errors, best practices in healthcare, and improving healthcare quality and patient outcomes.

She studied and took notes on each of these and summarized them into new ideas that were additive and complementary to her original four ideas.

First, the new research emphasized poor communication as a critical issue even more strongly than she had originally thought. Multiple healthcare professionals who depend upon verbal communication seemed to be transferring important information through a flawed electronic healthcare record system.

Second, Mary was surprised to learn that patients' inadequate knowledge about their own historical health conditions and records are now more influential than ever in causing medical errors. The most important cause of this is the inadequate availability of a consistent medical record known by the patient. She was astonished that in today's technology-centric world this would still be one of the major root causes of medical errors, but the statistics confirmed that this was the case.

Another cause of medical errors that she did not find surprising, given the pandemic, is staffing patterns and workflow issues leading to bedside staff being unable to provide proper care and to document the process. This problem is compounded by a high professional staff turnover rate.

Step 4: Mary's MegaCepts List

Mary's updated list is comprised of eight MegaCepts:

- **Inadequate checklists:** The lack of rigorous, accurate, and complete medical procedure checklists directly at the point of patient care has become an even more significant problem due to the proliferation of medical diagnoses and treatments. It's vital to improve these checklists and make them more accessible by employing best-practice information technology (IT) software and systems.

- **Poor communication:** Healthcare providers depend on good verbal communication, and yet they need to communicate through an imperfect electronic healthcare record system. It is important to share patient progress within each phase of hospital care, so the patient is "handed off" from medical team to medical team.

- **Inadequate information flow:** There is no objective measure of the specific steps of care that prevent poor outcomes. There is also no standard process of communication of information among the multiple medical professionals who take care of a patient. We need to provide a checklist of evidence-based steps that are objective as well as data points that all the medical professionals involved with a patient can access in real time during the entire caregiving process by, again, employing best-practice IT software and systems.

- **Poor human judgment:** The amount of medical knowledge doubles every two years, so assimilating evidence-based information is a challenge, especially due to differing levels of experience, knowledge, skill, and process understanding. We need to provide IT-based systems that provide medical professionals with accurate and current training and process understanding.

- **Patient-related factors:** Inadequate availability of a consistent medical record known by the patient is a complicating factor. We need real-time availability of patient medical records for all medical professionals at the point of patient care.

- **Organizational transfer of knowledge:** Inconsistent documentation results in incorrect or untimely applications of a care plan. We currently lack a standard method to collect data, such as a checklist, to guarantee that each treatment step occurs. We need to provide a common IT system with consistent and updated documentation of all treatment results and status.

- **Inadequate policies:** This is a combination of the inadequacies of certain processes as well as the staff being unaware of some hospital policies. We need to include policies as part of an IT-based system to inform medical professionals about the latest policies related to the current treatment situation.

- **Staffing patterns and workflow:** Current numbers of bedside staff are inadequate to provide proper care and to document the process. We need to increase medical professional time with the patient by reducing administrative load, especially in the area of updating patient records.

Mary was pleased with her MegaCepts list, since it incorporated her past thinking and augmented it with current medical-error information, especially related to pandemic-related inputs. She was also pleased by the clarity of her eight MegaCepts, due to the clear, organized structure of the process.

Mary's updated self-rating follows:

- Education on the topic: 9
- Understanding of the topic: 9
- Confidence about the topic: 9
- Ability to provide leadership on the topic: 9
- Current satisfaction regarding the topic: 9
- Total score: 45 versus 35 at the beginning of the process

Mary's updated scores all moved to nines. Her biggest reasons for the improvements included her review of new research and statistics on the subject and organizing the information in a structured way, so she could think about it and talk about it more easily.

So, despite already being an expert on the subject of medical errors, Mary's updated rating actually improved fairly dramatically. "I concluded that the structured MegaCepts process provided me and my colleagues with a clearer, more organized way to think about the subject of medical errors," Mary told me. "It also provides a foundation to continuously enhance our understanding with ongoing study and inclusion. Finally, that same structure provides a better way to communicate this subject to the most important participant, the patient."

Exercise

As you have seen, you can apply the MegaCepts process to a wide variety of topics, from everyday topics like being a parent to more complex ones like understanding AI and reducing medical errors.

I want to leave you with a short exercise. You have just read about how two experts, Ray and Mary, applied the MegaCepts process to further expand their expertise. Everyone has at least one area of expertise. Choose one that you feel particularly strong and confident about. This could come from your career, academic studies, or personal experiences. For example, you might be a high school math and science teacher or an expert swimmer or gardener. Update your expertise on that topic by applying the MegaCepts process to it, just like Ray and Mary did, and see what your greatest thoughts look like at the end. I predict that you will be both surprised and pleased with the result!

Brief Thoughts about Mary's MegaCepts Process and Improving Healthcare

Healthcare is the largest industry in the world and has a direct impact on the health and well-being of billions of people. Given the enormous impact of medical errors on world health, it is perhaps the single most important focus for improving healthcare. Mary's focus on increasing her knowledge on this subject is powerful in how it evolved from her beginning thoughts to her greatest thoughts at the end of the MegaCepts process. I'm sure you have gained some understanding on this important topic as well.

I am executive chairman of a digital heath software company that provides a best-practices, clinical decision support system to help solve the worldwide issue of reducing medical errors. The company is actively involved in and aligned with the United Nations (UN) Sustainable Development Goals (SDG) initiative, which is focused on improving seventeen important areas that support the world population. These areas include water, food, poverty, and so on. One of the most important areas is called SDG3 and is focused on world health and well-being. And one of its most important areas of focus is reducing medical errors.

SDG3 is attracting significant funding from a wide range of organizations. One powerful group is the 460 largest healthcare companies in the world that are being asked to invest 1 percent of their pension funds into the SDG3 initiative. That would be trillions of dollars. If you have an interest in learning more about this, search on this topic, and you will learn a lot more about the UN SDG in general and SDG3 in particular.

*"No law or ordinance is mightier
than understanding."*

—PLATO

Acting on the Greatest Thoughts of This Book

*"It is not enough to have a good mind;
the main thing is to use it well."*

—RENE DESCARTES

hope that by reading this book you have gained a greater appreciation of how important thinking is in your life. In the exercise at the end of Chapter 3, I asked you to answer four questions about yourself before reading this book:

- How important do you believe that thinking is in your life today?

- How much more important would you like thinking to be for you in the future?

- How would you rate yourself on how often and how well you think today?

- How important is it that you learn to think more and think better?

Now that you have read and thought about this book, how would you answer these questions right now? Take a few minutes to write down your thoughts, then compare your answers to your initial thoughts. Did the answers change? If so, why do you think that is?

Having read this book, I hope you have broadened your understanding of thinking and have a good sense of how the MegaCepts process can help you think smarter for a better life. Everyone, regardless of their "going-in knowledge," can apply this process to any topic and gain a much better understanding of that topic.

Better thinking should not be a burden, a chore, or a problem. It can be—and should be—an uplifting experience and an enduring process in your life. It should also be fun and fulfilling!

Remember this book's key themes:

- **Thinking is for everyone:** You don't have to be a genius to think better and more effectively, but you do need to commit to it and then have a simple and easy-to-use process to help facilitate your thinking.

- **Thinking should be focused:** This book proves that all subjects, from the simplest to the most complex, can be broken down into ten or fewer greatest thoughts, or MegaCepts.

- **Thinking can be easy:** This book provides an easy-to-learn, four-step process that anyone can use to better understand any subject, resulting in dramatically better thinking and the benefits from that thinking. This process was illustrated with several real-life examples in this book.

- **Thinking by using the MegaCepts process works:** I have been successfully using and teaching the MegaCepts process for over five decades with many positive results. I hope the examples you've now read will help you use the MegaCepts process to improve your own thinking dramatically.

Before we close let's try one more fun exercise. You have now read this book and understand what MegaCepts are and how to define them for any topic. So, please apply this process to define what you believe to be the thesis of and MegaCepts of this book. What are the greatest thoughts on thinking that this book conveyed to you? Think of the thesis as the single, most important point in your MegaCepts list.

Take a few minutes to write down your book thesis and MegaCepts before you read the following paragraphs, which present my ideas. Once you have written them down, then continue reading. I'll share with you what I think is the thesis for and the MegaCepts of this book, which follow.

This Book's Thesis

Mega Thinking, or great thinking, can be achieved by using a simple, powerful process to make better leadership decisions. This process enables you to define the ten or fewer MegaCepts, or greatest thoughts, on any topic. The ability to make better personal and professional leadership decisions leads to a more fulfilling and successful life.

MegaCepts of This Mega Thinking Book

- The human brain, and its capacity to think, is the most powerful and important capability for every person. It is even the sole reason why humans stay alive! For centuries, hundreds of world-renowned philosophers, scientists, and leaders have acknowledged the importance of thinking via their wisdom and famous quotations.

"All that is, is the result of what we have thought."

—GAUTAMA BUDDHA

Scientific research has confirmed that the brain thinks at the subconscious and conscious levels. This book is focused on providing a process to improve your conscious thinking in general and on more complex and important topics in particular.

"The whole of science is nothing more than a refinement of everyday thinking."

—ALBERT EINSTEIN

The MegaCepts process enables a person to establish the ten, or fewer, most important greatest thoughts on any topic. The process is simple, but powerful, in helping anyone to achieve great thinking on a topic.

"All that man achieves and all that he fails to achieve is the direct result of his own thoughts."

—JAMES ALLEN

There are numerous examples of complex and important topics where authorities have established ten or fewer greatest thoughts. Examples include the seven major religions, the eight major forms of government, and the three major branches of science. These greatest thoughts, essentially MegaCepts, enable better understanding of these topics. For example, the Ten Commandments provide a structured and valuable way to understand Christianity.

"As a man thinketh in his heart, so shall he be."

—PROVERBS 23:7

Studies confirm that despite the importance of thinking and the brain's powerful ability to think, many people do not think effectively and, in many cases, do not think at all. Many people consider that thinking about complex and important topics is both complicated and intimidating, so they choose not to do it, and most people lack an organized, structured process to achieve great thinking.

*"There is no expedient to which a man
will go to avoid the labor of thinking."*

—THOMAS EDISON

The MegaCepts process provides four steps that facilitate a person's ability to define the ten or fewer greatest thoughts on any topic: 1. Initial ideas, 2. Socialized ideas, 3. Research ideas, and 4. Final MegaCepts list.

*"A man that does not think for
himself does not think at all."*

—OSCAR WILDE

The best way to understand the MegaCepts process is to illustrate its use with real people, successfully applying it to actual topics. This book reviews six people who applied the MegaCepts process to the following topics: parenting teenagers, picking a college major, improving interpersonal skills, understanding AI, becoming an effective leader, and reducing medical errors.

"No problem can be solved until it is reduced to some simple form. The changing of a vague difficulty into a specific, concrete form is a very essential element in thinking."

—J. P. MORGAN

Achieving great thinking in making better leadership decisions will result in your personal, educational, and professional life being better and more fulfilling..

"The more man meditates on good thoughts, the better will be his world and the world at large."

—CONFUCIUS

The author has been successfully using and teaching the MegaCepts approach for over five decades. He has used it to materially benefit his personal, academic, and professional life and has coached thousands of others to do the same. This book is his attempt to provide the benefits of this approach to thinking to millions more people to make their lives better.

> *"People are about as happy as they
> make up their minds to be."*

—ABRAHAM LINCOLN

Create Your Final List of MegaCepts for This Book

Now refer to your initial list and the above list of MegaCepts for this book to create your own, final MegaCepts list, which will be the best for you, since your final list represents your own thinking. Make copies of your MegaCepts list and put them where they will remind you to keep finding the greatest thoughts on all topics.

Now that you have finished this book, I welcome any comments and questions you might have; please feel free to send an email to me at Dave@MegaThinkingBook.com.

I also encourage you to review the appendixes for further reading and insight on the topic of thinking. Appendix 1 contains an expanded list of notable quotations on thinking, many of which I find particularly stimulating, challenging, motivating, and witty. You will find a list of additional books and articles on thinking in Appendix 2. You will also find appendixes that review in more detail the interesting subjects of religion and government and include the greatest thoughts for each, as defined by established authorities.

Please visit www.MegaThinkingBook.com. You can share your thoughts on thinking and interact with others on your favorite topics. Please also share your experiences and successes with the MegaCepts process (either by name or anonymously). At the website, you can find out about my latest books, articles, and lectures that further develop the power and scope of the MegaCepts process.

As your new Coach, I wish you tremendous success and satisfaction with your new and improved ability to think smarter and make better leadership decisions, resulting in a better life. And thank you for reading my book!

Quotations about Thinking from World Authorities

This appendix lists over one hundred quotations about thinking from famous, respected authors. It includes quotations presented earlier in this book as well as additional quotations. I have organized these according to the six key impacts and requirements of thinking that I discussed in Chapter 3:

- **Thinking defines us:** Thinking is an innate capability of mankind. If properly applied (or not), it is a primary factor in defining who we are.

- **Thinking educates us:** Improved thinking is also learning, leading to better knowledge and wisdom on any topic. This is especially true for more challenging and complex topics and issues.

- **Thinking impacts our success:** Your ability to think, and your actual application of thinking, will have a major impact on your success or failure in all aspects of your life, including personally, educationally, and professionally.

- **Thinking has other personal benefits:** Thinking provides other mental and emotional benefits, including higher confidence, better self-image, more complete self-fulfillment, and even increased happiness. Better thinking helps you get on top of any topic and manage it effectively.

- **Thinking requires you to actively and effectively use your brain:** Many, and perhaps most, people do not think as much as they should and could. Many literally don't think at all on more complex topics. Even those who do think often think less effectively than they could and should. You need to turn your brain on, just like you need to turn your computer on.

- **Thinking needs commitment and discipline:** Thinking might seem complex and intimidating, but it doesn't have to be. You can learn to think better, but you need to want to, and you need to apply yourself. Using an organized and structured way to think is the best way to think better about any topic.

- **Witty, fun, and satirical quotations:** Some of these are just fun and witty. Others are satirical to make a point.

Thinking Defines Us

- **Ambrose Bierce:** *1842–1914.* American short-story writer and journalist. "The art of thinking and reasoning is in strict accordance with the limitations and incapacities of the human understanding."

- **Gautama Buddha:** *563–483 BC.* A monk, mendicant, and sage on whose teachings Buddhism was founded.

  - "With our thoughts we make the world."

  - "All that is, is the result of what we have thought."

  - "We are what we think."

  - "What we think, we become."

- **Marcus Tullius Cicero:** *106–43 BC.* A Roman statesman, orator, lawyer, and philosopher, considered to be one of Rome's greatest orators and prose stylists. "To think is to live."

- **Rene Descartes:** *1596–1650.* French philosopher, mathematician, and scientist.

  - "I think therefore I am." *Discourse on the Method*, 1637.

  - "Except for our own thoughts, there is nothing absolutely in our power."

  - "Nurture your mind with great thoughts."

- **Ralph Waldo Emerson:** *1803–1882*. American essayist, lecturer, philosopher, and poet. "Thoughts rule the World." Complete quote: "Great men are they who see that spiritual is stronger than any material force, that thoughts rule the world. No hope so bright but is the beginning of its own fulfillment." Progress of Culture Speech, Phi Beta Kappa Address. July 18, 1867.

- **Benjamin Franklin:** *1706–1790*. American polymath and one of the founding fathers of the United States. He was a leading author, printer, political theorist, politician, Freemason, postmaster, scientist, humorist, civic activist, statesman, and diplomat.

  - "To cease to think creatively is little different from ceasing to live."

  - Jesus: 4 BC–33 AD. The critical figure of Christianity. "As you think, so shall you be." The Bible, Proverbs 2.

  - Henry Wadsworth Longfellow: 1807–1882. American poet and educator. "Thought takes man out of servitude, into freedom."

- **Plato:** *428–348 BC*. Classical Greek philosopher and founder of the Academy in Athens, the first institution of higher learning in the Western world. He is widely considered the pivotal figure in the development of Western philosophy.

- "Thinking: the talking of the soul with itself."

- "When the mind is thinking it is talking to itself."

- **The Bible, Proverbs 23:7:** "As a man thinketh in his heart, so is he."

- **Socrates:** *470–399 BC.* Greek philosopher and one of the founders of Western philosophy.

  - "To find yourself, think for yourself."

  - "Know thyself."

  - "The only good is knowledge and the only evil is ignorance."

- **Virgil:** *70–19 BC.* One of Rome's greatest poets. "They can do all because they think they can."

Thinking Educates Us

- **Aristotle:** *384–322 BC.* Ancient Greek philosopher who, along with Plato, is considered a father of Western philosophy. "It is the mark of an educated mind to entertain a thought without accepting it."

- **Confucius:** *551–479 BC.* A Chinese teacher, editor, politician, and philosopher of the Spring and Autumn period of Chinese history.

  - "Learning without thought is labor lost; thought without learning is perilous."

  - "He who learns but does not think is lost. He who thinks but does not learn is in great danger."

- **Mahatma Gandhi:** *1869–1948.* Indian activist who was the leader of India's independence movement against British rule. "Those who think need no teachers."

- **John Locke:** *1632–1704.* English philosopher and physician. "Reading furnishes the mind only with materials of knowledge; it is thinking that makes what we read ours."

- **Plato:** *428–348 BC.* Classical Greek philosopher and founder of the Academy in Athens, the first institution of higher learning in the Western world. He is widely considered the pivotal figure in the development of Western philosophy. "No law or ordinance is mightier than understanding."

- **Xun Kuang (Xunzi):** *313–238 BC.* Chinese Confucian philosopher who contributed to the Hundred Schools of Thought. "I once tried thinking for an entire day, but I found it less valuable than one moment of study."

Thinking Impacts Our Success

- **James Allen:** *1864–1912*. British philosophic writer known for his inspirational books and poetry and as a pioneer of the self-help movement. His most famous book is *As a Man Thinketh*, which has been a source of inspiration to motivational and self-help authors. "All that a man achieves and all that he fails to achieve is the direct result of his own thoughts."

- **Confucius:** *551–479 BC*. A Chinese teacher, editor, politician, and philosopher of the Spring and Autumn period of Chinese history: "The superior man thinks always of virtue; the common man thinks of comfort. The superior man thinks of sanctions of law; the small man thinks of favors he may receive." *The Analects*.

- **Albert Einstein:** *1879–1955*. German-born theoretical physicist who developed the theory of relativity, $E=MC^2$. His work is known for its influence on the philosophy of science.

  - "The world as we have created it is a process of our thinking. It cannot be changed without changing our thinking."

  - "Any man who reads too much and uses his own brain too little falls into lazy habits of thinking."

  - "I think and think for months and years. Ninety-nine times, the conclusion is false. The hundredth time I am right."

- **Ralph Waldo Emerson:** *1803–1882.* American essayist, lecturer, philosopher, and poet. "The ancestor of every action is a thought."

- **Khalil Gibran:** *1883–1931.* Lebanese American writer, poet, and visual artist: "Faith is an oasis in the heart which will never be reached by the caravan of thinking."

- **Johann Wolfgang von Goethe:** *1749–1832.* German writer and statesman. "Thinking is easy, acting is difficult, and to put one's thoughts into action is the most difficult thing in the world."

- **George S. Patton:** *1885–1945.* US Army General during World War II: "If everyone is thinking alike, then somebody isn't thinking."

- **Henry David Thoreau:** *1817–1862,* American essayist, poet, historian, philosopher, abolitionist, tax resistor, development critic, surveyor, and historian. "If there was one life skill everyone on the planet needed it was the ability to think with critical objectivity."

- **Unknown author:** "Invest a few moments in thinking, it will pay good interest."

- **Henry Van Dyke:** *1852–1933.* American author, educator, and clergyman. "No amount of energy will take the place of thought. A strenuous life with its eyes shut is a kind of wild insanity."

- **Oscar Wilde:** *1854–1900.* Irish playwright and poet. "A man that does not think for himself does not think at all."

Thinking Has Other Personal Benefits

- **Marcus Aurelius:** *121–180 AD.* Roman emperor, called "the philosopher," and a leading practitioner of Stoicism.

  - "The happiness of your life depends on the quality of your thoughts."

  - "Very little is needed to make a happy life; it is all within yourself, in your way of thinking."

- **Confucius:** *551–479 BC.* A Chinese teacher, editor, politician, and philosopher of the Spring and Autumn period of Chinese history: "The more man meditates on good thoughts, the better will be his world and the world at large."

- **Henry Ford:** *1863–1947.* American captain of industry, business magnate, and founder of Ford Motor Company. "The more you think, the more time you have."

Thinking Requires You to Actively and Effectively Use Your Brain

- **Henri Bergson:** *1848–1941*. French philosopher. "Think like a man of action, act like a man of thought." Said in a speech at Descartes Conference, 1937.

- **William Bragg:** *1862–1942*. English physicist and mathematician. "The important thing in science is not so much to obtain new facts as to discover new ways to think about them."

- **Thomas Edison:** *1847–1931*. American inventor and businessman who has been described as America's greatest inventor. His inventions include the phonograph, motion picture camera, and electric light bulb. "Five percent of the people think; ten percent of the people think they think; and the other eighty-five percent would rather die than think."

- **Ralph Waldo Emerson:** *1803–1882*. American essayist, lecturer, philosopher, and poet. "A sect or party is an elegant incognito devised to save man from the vexation of thinking."

- **Henry Ford:** *1863–1947*. American captain of industry, business magnate, and founder of Ford Motor Company. "Thinking is the hardest work there is, which is probably why so few engage in it."

- **Oliver Wendell Holmes:** *1841–1935*. American jurist who served as associate justice of the Supreme Court and acting chief justice. "Fame usually comes to those who are thinking about something else."

- **Soren Kierkegaard:** *1813–1855*. Danish philosopher, theologian, poet, social critic, and religious author widely considered to be the first existentialist philosopher. "People demand freedom of speech as a compensation for the freedom of thought which they seldom use."

- **George Bernard Shaw:** *1856–1950*. Irish playwright, critic, polemicist, and political activist. "Few people think more than two or three times a year. I have made an international reputation for myself by thinking once or twice a week."

- **Oscar Wilde:** *1854–1900*. Irish playwright and poet. "If you cannot write well, you cannot think well, others will do your thinking for you."

Thinking Needs Commitment and Discipline

- **James M. Barrie:** *1860–1937*. Scottish novelist and playwright. "I have always found that the man whose second thoughts are good is worth watching."

- **Karl Von Clausewitz:** *1780–1831.* A Prussian general and military theorist who stressed the moral, psychological, and political aspects of war. "Principles and rules are intended to provide a thinking man with a frame of reference."

- **Rene Descartes:** *1596–1650.* French philosopher, mathematician, and scientist. "It is not enough to have a good mind; the main thing is to use it well."

- **Thomas Edison:** *1847–1931.* American inventor and businessman who has been described as America's greatest inventor. His inventions include the phonograph, motion picture camera, and electric light bulb. "The best thinking has been done in solitude. The worst has been done in turmoil."

- **Albert Einstein:** *1879–1954.* German-born theoretical physicist who developed the theory of relativity, $E=MC^2$. His work is known for its influence on the philosophy of science.

  - "We cannot solve our problems with the same thinking we used when we created them."

  - "Figuring out how to think about the problem." This was his response when asked what single event was most helpful in developing his famous breakthrough in the theory of relativity.

- "The whole of science is nothing more than a refinement of everyday thinking." From "Physics and Reality" in the *Journal of the Franklin Institute*, Vol. 221, Issue 3, March 1936.

- "The important thing is to not stop questioning." From "Death of a Genius," *Life* magazine, May 2, 1955.

- "A new type of thinking is essential if mankind is to survive and move to higher levels."

- **Ralph Waldo Emerson:** *1803–1882.* American essayist, lecturer, philosopher, and poet. "In every work of genius, we recognize our own rejected thoughts: They come back to us with a certain alienated majesty." From his essay "Self-Reliance," 1841.

- **Abraham Lincoln:** *1809–1865.* American statesman and sixteenth president of the United States. "When I get ready to talk to people, I spend two thirds of the time thinking what they want to hear and one third thinking about what I want to say."

- **J. P. Morgan:** *1837–1913.* American financier and banker.

- "No problem can be solved until it is reduced to some simple form. The changing of a vague difficulty into a specific, concrete form is a very essential element in thinking."

- "I'll be more enthusiastic about encouraging thinking outside the box if there's evidence of any thinking going on inside the box."

- **Francois Duc de La Rochefoucauld:** *1613–1680.* French author of maxims and memoirs. "Our minds are lazier than our bodies."

- **Franklin D. Roosevelt:** *1882–1945.* American statesman and thirty-second president of the United States. "I am neither bitter nor cynical but I do wish there was less immaturity in political thinking."

- **Socrates:** *470–399 BC.* Greek philosopher and one of the founders of Western philosophy. "I cannot teach anybody anything, I can only make them think."

- **Voltaire:** *1694–1778.* French enlightenment writer, historian, and philosopher famous for his advocacy of freedom of religion, freedom of speech, and separation of church and state.

  - "No problem can stand the assault of sustained thinking."

  - "Dare to think for yourself."

  - "Think for yourselves and let others enjoy the privilege to do so too."

Witty, Fun, and Satirical Quotations:

- **Christian N. Bovee:** *1820-1904.* Epigrammatic New York City writer who wrote *Institutions and Summaries of Thought.* "Few minds wear out; more rust out."

- **Luther Burbank:** *1849-1926.* American botanist, horticulturist, and pioneer in agricultural science. "It is well for people who think, to change their minds occasionally in order to keep them clean."

- **Bruce Calvert:** *1866-1940.* American author. "Believing is easier than thinking. Hence so many more believers than thinkers."

- **Thomas Edison: 1847-1931.** American inventor and businessman who has been described as America's greatest inventor. His inventions include the phonograph, motion picture camera, and electric light bulb. "There is no expedient to which a man will not go to avoid the labor of thinking."

- **Ralph Waldo Emerson:** *1803-1882.* American essayist, lecturer, philosopher, and poet.

  - "If a man sits down to think, he is immediately asked if he has a headache."

  - "What is the hardest task in the world? To think."

- **Henry Ford:** *1863–1947*. American captain of industry, business magnate, and founder of Ford Motor Company: "Whether you think you can, or think you can't, you're right."

- **Jonathan Lockwood Huie:** American philosopher. "Thinking is what most people resort to when all else fails."

- **William James:** *1842–1910*. American philosopher and psychologist known as the father of American psychology. "A great many people think they are thinking when they are merely rearranging their prejudices."

- **George Kirkpatrick:** *1867–1937*. American writer. "Nature gave man two ends—one to sit on and one to think with. Ever since then, man's success or failure has been dependent on which one he uses most."

- **Abraham Lincoln:** *1809–1865*. American statesman and sixteenth president of the United States. "People are about as happy as they make up their minds to be."

- **Unknown author:**

  - "Thinking is the greatest torture in the world for most people."

  - "I don't think inside the box and I don't think outside the box . . . I don't even know where the box is."

- "Some minds are like concrete, thoroughly mixed and permanently set."

- "I'm trying to think how I can think of what I want to think."

- "My train of thought derailed. There were no survivors."

- "The only reason people get lost in thought is because it's unfamiliar territory."

- "Your mind needs exercise as much as your body does. That's why I think of jogging every day."

- "If everyone knew what I was thinking, I would get punched in the face a lot."

- "My mind not only wanders, sometimes it leaves completely."

- "I get tired from just thinking of everything I have to do."

- "If you make people think they're thinking, they'll love you; but if you really make them think, they'll hate you."

- "When all else fails, try thinking."

- "Invest a few moments in thinking—it will pay good interest."

Further Reading on Thinking

The *5 Elements of Effective Thinking* by Edward B. Burger and Michael Starbird. 2012. 168 pages. Princeton University Press.

- Explains how people can attain success by thinking more effectively.

- Offers strategies, stories, plans for action, and methods for understanding problems in the world.

- Allows readers to understand the power of failure, ask better questions, rethink their worldview, and see how they can change for the better.

The 7 Habits of Highly Effective People by Stephen R. Covey. 1988. 464 pages. Simon and Schuster.

- Helps people learn how to better solve personal and professional problems.

- Offers a set of steps for people to live lives full of virtue while still being successful.

- The seven habits include: be proactive; begin with the end in mind; put first things first; think win-win; seek first to understand, then to be understood; synergize; sharpen the saw.

The Art of Thinking Clearly by Rolf Dobelli. 2014. 384 pages. Harper.

- Helps people avoid "cognitive errors" and make better choices.

- Helps people figure out what to ignore and what to focus on in their lives.

As a Man Thinketh by James Allen. 1903 and 1993, 80 pages. Barbour.

- Awakens people to the discovery that they are the masters of themselves.

- The Bible verse "As a man thinketh, so he is" is a reality within the power of each person to discover and create his own happiness.

A Better Way to Think by H. Norman Wright. 2003. 145 pages. Oxford University Press.

- Relates how positive thoughts can change your life.

- Shows readers how to truly bring every thought captive under Christ, thereby freeing themselves from patterns of self-talk that have stymied their personal and spiritual growth for years.

Change Your Thinking, Change Your life by Brian Tracy. 2003. 288 pages. Wiley.

- Tells how to unlock your full potential for success and achievement.

- Provides a step-by-step system to transform your thinking about yourself and your potential, enabling you to achieve greater success in every area of your life.

Critical Thinking Beginners Guide by Carl Patterson. 2020. 190 pages. Tons of Tomes Ltd.

- Teaches readers how reasoning by logic improves effective problem solving.

- Gives the reader tools to think smarter, level up their intuition to reach their potential, and grow their mindfulness.

Critical Thinking: Tools for Taking Charge of Your Professional and Personal Life by Richard Paul and Linda Elder. 2002 and 2020. 528 pages. Pearson and Rowman & Littlefield.

- Helps people use better thinking to achieve their goals.

- Enables people to assess and improve their ways of thinking.

- Introduces six distinct stages of thinking.

Intelligent Thinking by Sam Bathla. 2019. 185 pages. Independently published.

- Teaches readers to power up their brains.

- Coaches readers in overcoming thinking errors, learning advanced techniques to think intelligently, and making smarter choices.

- Teaches how readers can become the best versions of themselves.

The Logical Thinking Process by H. William Dettmer. 2007. 448 pages. American Society for Quality, Quality Press.

- Offers a systems approach to complex problem solving.

- Teaches a whole new approach to building and applying logic trees.

The Magic of Thinking Big by David J. Schwartz. 1959 and 1987. 238 pages. Cornerstone.

- Helps people achieve the most out of their lives: financial security, power and influence, the ideal job, satisfying relationships, and a rewarding, happy life.

- Proves that talent and intelligence are not necessary for success.

- Teaches that it is necessary to understand the habit of thinking and to strive for the following:

  - Have a mindset in which you believe in yourself.

  - Have motivation that will help you overcome challenges.

  - Demonstrate confidence, attitude, respect for others, and careful planning.

Master Your Mind by Marcel Dansei. 2020. 152 pages. Rockridge Press.

- Provides critical-thinking exercises and activities to boost your brain power and think smarter.

- Sharpens critical thinking skills and tells how to power your brain for life.

Mindset: The New Psychology of Success by Carol S. Dweck. 2007. 320 pages. Random House.

- Teaches how success in almost every part of people's lives is influenced by how people think about their talents and abilities.

- Explains that a fixed mindset (a belief that one can't change) makes it harder for people to be prosperous in life.

- In the book, Dweck says that "With the right mindset, you can motivate those you lead, teach, and love—to transform their lives and your own."

The Power of Positive Thinking by Dr. Norman Vincent Peale. 1952 and 2002. 240 pages. Simon and Schuster.

- Describes a way to achieve fulfillment in life with a message of faith and inspiration.

- Helps people believe in themselves to achieve success.

- Shows how to stop worrying, improve relationships, have power/determination, and take control of your life.

Powerful Thinking by Joyce Meyer. 2021. 176 pages. Faith Words.

- Outlines a flexible program to turn thoughts into habits and habits into success.

- Sections include the power of a positive you, keeping your attitude at the right altitude, the power of perspective, and more power to you.

The Rules of Thinking by Richard Templar. 2019. 222 pages. Pearson Education Ltd.

- Discover the Rules of Thinking, a brand-new set of rules that allows you to discover how to think well, make better decisions, and solve problems.

- These rules are the guiding principles that show you how to make wiser decisions, stop procrastinating, know when to compromise, avoid mistakes, find other options, think well with others, stop obsessing about things, keep your brain active, be more creative, and have happy, healthy thoughts.

Six Thinking Hats by Edward de Bono. 1985 and 2008. 177 pages. Little Brown & Co. and Penguin Books Ltd.

- Defines and explains six different approaches to thinking that are categorized by different colored hats: blue—organization and planning, white—facts and information, green—ideas and creativity, yellow—benefits and value, red—feelings and instincts, black—risks and cautions.

Smart Thinking by Art Markman. 2012. 272 pages. Tarcher Perigee.

- Describes a three-part formula that shows how smart thinking is different from innate intelligence and explains how to learn and how to use your knowledge. The formula includes smart habits, right knowledge, and high-quality knowledge.

- Helps people develop smart habits, acquire useful knowledge, and use the knowledge to succeed.

- Helps people understand their minds and memories, how to convey information, how to better understand the world, and how to define and understand problems.

Think to Win: Understanding the Power of Strategic Thinking by John Manfredi, Paul Butler, and Peter Klein. 2015. 240 pages. McGraw-Hill.

- Redefines, demystifies, and simplifies great thinking and decision-making for any business, small or large.

- Strips out all the complexity and offers a system that works at an individual level and throughout the organization.

Think and Grow Rich by Napoleon Hill. 1937 and 2005. 320 pages. Tarcher Perigee.

- Outlines the author's philosophy of success.

- Describes sixteen laws for achieving success and provides readers with thirteen principles for doing so.

- Shows how desire, faith, and persistence can lead to success if one also focuses on long-term goals.

Think Smarter by Michael Kallet. 2014. 240 pages. Wiley.

- Teaches how to use critical thinking to improve problem-solving and decision-making skills.

- Allows readers to learn critical thinking techniques for better decisions, problem solving, and innovation.

Thinking, Fast and Slow by Daniel Kahneman. 2013. 512 pages. Farrar, Straus, and Stow.

- Shows how thinking is composed of two systems:

  - System 1: fast, intuitive, emotional

  - System 2: slower, deliberative, logical

- Better thinking, decisions, and more success will result from understanding when/how people use each of these systems.

Articles

- "7 Ways to Improve Your Critical Thinking Skills" by Ransom Patterson (www.collegeinfogeek.com)

- "10 Ways to Be a Better Thinker" by Jonah Lehrer (www. realsimple.com)

- "22 tips to Think Better" (www.lifehack.org)

- "How to Exercise Your Brain for Better Thinking Skills" (www.wikihow.com)

- "How to Think Better: The Top 8 Tips from the Last 2500 Years" by Henrik Edberg (www.positivityblog.com)

- "You've Been Thinking All Wrong: Here's how to Think Better" by Shane Parrish (www.observer.com)

The MegaCepts of Six
Major Religions

I n this appendix and in Appendix 4, I will provide examples of MegaCepts defined by authorities on each subject. None of these sources use the term "MegaCepts," but I am equating this term to the authority's definition of the basic principles of the topic. While you do not need to thoroughly read every example in these two appendixes, I encourage to read through enough to recognize that all topics can be expressed via MegaCepts and that many complex topics have already been defined by prior authorities. This appendix presents the MegaCepts of six major religions, and Appendix 4 presents the MegaCepts of eight forms of government.

Most if not all religions have well-established principles that represent the MegaCepts of their faith. In the introduction, I used Christianity as an example. Below are the MegaCepts of six other major world religions: Buddhism, Islam, Confucianism, Judaism, Hinduism, and Taoism.

Buddhism

Buddhism originated in India by Buddha (Gautama) and spread to China, Burma, Japan, Tibet, and parts of Southeast Asia. Buddhism holds that life is full of suffering caused by desire, and that the way to end this suffering is through the enlightenment that enables one to halt the endless sequence of births and deaths to which one is otherwise subject. Buddhism is the world's fourth largest religion, with over 520 million followers or over 7 percent of the global population known as Buddhists. The core beliefs are the Four Noble Truths, the Noble Eightfold Path, and the Five Precepts.

The Buddhists' three core beliefs represent three different ways to express the MegaCepts of Buddhism.

- The Four Noble Truths:

    - Dissatisfaction and suffering exist and are universally experienced.

    - Desire and attachment are the causes of dissatisfaction and suffering.

    - There is an end to dissatisfaction and suffering.

    - The end can be obtained by journeying on the Noble Eightfold Path.

- The Noble Eightfold Path:

    - Right View/Understanding: See things as they are without delusions or distortions, for all things change.

    - Right Thinking: Decide to set a life on the correct path.

    - Right Speech: Abstain from lies and deceptions, backbiting, idle babble, and abusive speech.

    - Right Conduct: Practice selfless conduct that reflects the highest statement of the life you want to live.

- Right Livelihood: Earn a living that does not hurt living things.

- Right Effort: Seek to make a balance between the exertion of following the spiritual path and a moderate life that is not overzealous.

- Right Mindfulness: Become intensely aware of all the states in body, feeling, and mind.

- Right Concentration: Deep meditation to lead to a higher state of consciousness and enlightenment.

- Five Precepts:

  - I undertake the precept to refrain from destroying living creatures.

  - I understand the precept to refrain from taking that which is not given.

  - I understand the precept to refrain from sexual misconduct.

  - I understand the precept to refrain from incorrect speech.

  - I understand the precept to refrain from intoxicants.

"All that is, is the result of what we have thought."

—GAUTAMA BUDDHA

Islam

There are 1.6 billion Muslims, which represent 23 percent of the Earth's population. Islam was first preached by the Prophet Muhammad during the 600s on the Arabian Peninsula after he said he had a spiritual conversation with God. He preached the founding beliefs to a small group of core followers, eventually spreading throughout the Middle East, India, Southeast Asia, Africa, and even parts of Europe. In Arabic, *Islam* means to "surrender to Allah" (the Arabic word for God). The core belief of the religion is that Allah is the creator and controller of the world, meaning that people have a duty to follow his will. The Koran is the sacred book by Muhammad revealing what Allah told him, and this forms the core of the Islamic religion.

Key MegaCepts groups:

- Six Articles of Faith:

    - The belief in one God

- The belief in angels

- The belief in prophets of God

- The belief in revealed books of God

- The belief in the Day of Judgment

- The belief in destiny and divine decree

- The Five Pillars of Islam, or the basic duties of a devout Muslim:

  - The declaration of faith in only one God

  - Prayer five times per day

  - Charity to help the poor and needy

  - Fasting during the holy month of Ramadan

  - The Hajj pilgrimage to Mecca once in every capable person's lifetime

- Core Teachings of Prophet Muhammad (Sources: www. IslamReligion.com, www.PEWForum.org)

  - "Actions are judged by the intention behind them."

- "God is pure and does not accept anything unless it is pure, and God has commanded the faithful with what He commanded the prophets."

- "Part of a person's good observance of Islam is to leave aside what does not concern him."

- "A person cannot be a complete believer unless he loves for his brother what he loves for himself."

- "One should not harm himself or others."

- "Don't let your focus in this life be to amass worldly gain, and God will love you. Don't be concerned with what people have, and they will love you."

Confucianism

Some experts consider Confucianism as a way of life and philosophy rather than a religion, but Confucianism does have many aspects of a religion. Confucianism first spread by Confucius in China to his followers in the sixth and fifth century BCE and spread throughout East Asia over time. Confucianism is built around the appreciation of ancestors and centering one's beliefs around humans themselves; the family is made the center in life and comes before individuals. It is possible to adhere to other religions while still observing Confucian ideals. Confucianism was the interpretation of the beliefs held by the Zhou dynasty.

Key MegaCepts groups:

- The Five Virtues:

  - *Ren*—humaneness, or compassion for others (people and animals); love, mercy, and humanity

  - *Yi*—honesty, righteousness

  - *Li*—property, correct behavior

  - *Zhi*—wisdom, knowledge

  - *Xin*—fidelity, sincerity

- Six Key Virtues (similar to those above):

  - *Li*—ritual, property, etiquette

  - *Hsiao*—love within the family between parents and children

  - *Yi*—righteousness

  - *Xin*—honesty, trustworthiness

  - *Jen*—benevolence, humaneness; the highest virtue in Confucianism

  - *Chung*—loyalty to the state

- The Five Cardinal Relations:

  - Sovereign to subject

  - Father to son

  - Elder brother to younger brother

  - Husband to wife

  - Friend to friend

Judaism

There are fourteen million Jewish people, which make up 0.2 percent of the world's population. This religion was developed by the Hebrew people in the Middle East four thousand years ago. Abraham and later prophets had spiritual revelations that told them there was only one God, unlike the polytheistic religions common at the time. Judaism is centered around the teachings of the prophets Abraham, Moses, and others, and it concerns many aspects of daily life. Jews believe in the Torah, their holy book, and that they must follow God's laws governing life.

Key MegaCepts groups:

- The Ten Commandments, according to the Torah:

  - Worship no other God but me.

- Do not make images to worship.

- Do not misuse the name of God.

- Observe the Sabbath Day. Keep it Holy.

- Honor and respect your father and mother.

- Do not murder.

- Do not commit adultery.

- Do not steal.

- Do not accuse anyone falsely. Do not tell lies about other people.

- Do not envy other's possessions.

- Maimonides' Thirteen Principles of Jewish Faith written out in the Mishnah (a book holy to the Jewish people):

  - The belief in the existence of the God, the Creator

  - The belief in God's absolute and unparalleled unity

  - The belief that God is incorporeal; God will not be affected by any physical occurrences, such as movement or rest or dwelling

- The belief that God is eternal

- The imperative to worship God and no false gods; all prayer should be directed only to God

- The belief that God communicates with man through prophecy and that this prophecy is true

- The belief in the primacy of the prophecy of Moses

- The belief in the divine origin of the Torah—both the written and the oral (the *Talmud*)

- The belief in the immutability of the Torah

- The belief in God's omniscience and providence, that God knows the thoughts and deeds of man

- The belief in divine reward and retribution

- The belief in the arrival of the Messiah and the messianic era

- The belief in the resurrection of the dead

Hinduism

There are one billion Hindus, amounting to 15 percent of the world's population. Hinduism originated in India during the second millennium BCE or earlier, and some consider it to be the oldest religion in the world that is still practiced today. It is not composed of just one type of philosophy, belief, or set of rituals. Hinduism can be summed up as a set of beliefs with the goal of well-being and locating, removing, or appeasing sources of pain in life. Hindus believe there is a supreme God, represented by multiple deities. They believe in a cycle of birth, death, and rebirth governed by karma, and they believe the soul is reborn depending on the way a person lives. The most important holy texts are the Vedas, and there are derivations of this text. One single person did not found Hinduism; it is a compilation of many similar belief systems.

Key MegaCepts groups:

- The Nine Beliefs of Hinduism:

    - Hindus believe in one, all-pervasive Supreme Being who is both immanent and transcendent, both Creator and Unmanifest Reality.

    - Hindus believe in the divinity of the four Vedas, the world's most ancient scripture, and venerate the Agamas. They believe these primordial hymns are God's word and the bedrock of Sanatana Dharma, the eternal religion.

    - Hindus believe the universe undergoes endless cycles of creation, preservation, and dissolution.

    - Hindus believe in karma, the law of cause and effect, by

which each individual creates their own destiny by their thoughts, words, and deeds.

- Hindus believe the soul reincarnates, evolving through many births until all karmas have been resolved, and moksha, liberation from the cycle of rebirth, is attained. Not a single soul will be deprived of this destiny.

- Hindus believe divine beings exist in unseen worlds and that temple worship, rituals, sacraments, and personal devotionals create a communion with these devas and gods.

- Hindus believe an enlightened master, or *satguru*, is essential to know the Transcendent Absolute, as are personal discipline, good conduct, purification, pilgrimage, self-inquiry, meditation, and surrender in God.

- Hindus believe all life is sacred, to be loved and revered, and therefore practice *ahimsa*—noninjury, in thought, word, and deed.

- Hindus believe no religion teaches the only way to salvation above all others but that all genuine paths are facets of God's Light, deserving tolerance and understanding.

Taoism

There are twenty million followers worldwide, though some estimates are as high as 400 million. Taoism began in China two thousand years ago, and it continues today primarily in China and Taiwan. Taoism synthesized many of the earlier philosophies and religions in China. Zhang Daoling created the first Taoist school of thought. Taoism is based around the Tao (or Dao) or "the Way," which is the Taoist idea of the universe. The Tao is not a God, but Taoists worship multiple deities that are related to the Tao, based around the unifying opposites of Yin and Yang. They believe the world is made up of these complementary forces. Other main ideas of Taoism include harmony and union with nature, gaining spiritual immortality, becoming virtuous, and developing one's character.

Key MegaCepts groups:

- Central Taoist beliefs:

  - The Tao is the natural order of all things, the underlying life force of the universe.

  - One should accept both the good and bad parts of one's life.

  - The Three Jewels should be central: courage, generosity, and leadership.

  - One's life should be natural and simple, with no unnecessary or artificial parts.

- Everything in the world is in a constant cycle.

- Everything in life should follow a natural course and maintain spontaneity.

- Love and restraint should always be practiced.

- To be happy, be true to oneself.

- Show compassion to all, and honor life.

- Another set of key Taoist beliefs:

  - The universe is governed by the Tao, which creates all things.

  - Life is the greatest of all possessions. The goal of every human is to achieve a deep bond with the Tao.

  - Live in simplicity and let all things naturally take their own course.

  - Despise pomp and glory.

The MegaCepts of Eight Major Forms of Government

"Too often we enjoy the comfort of opinion without the discomfort of thought."

—JOHN F. KENNEDY

Depending on one's source, there are somewhere between twenty-three and sixty forms of government in the world. Each has well-established principles that represent the MegaCepts of its approach. Let's examine the MegaCepts of democratic republicanism, communism, socialism, anarchy, monarchy, oligarchy, theocracy, and totalitarianism.

Democratic Republicanism

The largest and most successful democratic republic in the world is the United States. Two parts of the US Constitution, the supreme law of the US, capture the key MegaCepts of the US democratic republic:

- The Constitution's seven original articles:

    - Article One: Describes congress, the legislative branch of the federal government.

    - Article Two: Describes the office of the president, the executive branch of the federal government.

    - Article Three: Describes the court system including the Supreme Court, the judicial branch of the federal government.

    - Article Four: Outlines the relations among the states and between each state and the federal government.

- Article Five: Outlines the process for amending the Constitution.

- Article Six: Establishes the Constitution, and all federal laws and treaties of the US that are made according to it, to be the supreme law of the land.

- Article Seven: Describes the process for establishing the proposed new frame of government.

- The Ten Amendments to the Constitution, called the Bill of Rights. These rights describe limits on governmental power:

  - Amendment I: The right to freedom of religion, speech, assembly, and to petition the government for redress of grievances.

  - Amendment II: The right to have state militias and for people to bear arms.

  - Amendment III: Soldiers may not be quartered in any house without the consent of the owner.

  - Amendment IV: The right of the people to be secure and not be subject to unreasonable searches and seizures.

  - Amendment V: The right to presumption of innocence for crimes unless via presentment of indictment by a jury.

- Amendment VI: The right to a speedy and public trial by an impartial jury.

- Amendment VII: Common law cases decided by a jury may not be appealed to higher courts.

- Amendment VIII: Excessive bail will not be required, and there will be no cruel and unusual punishment.

- Amendment IX: The enumeration in the Constitution of certain rights shall not be construed to deny or disparage other rights retained by the people.

- Amendment X: The powers not delegated to the US by the Constitution, nor prohibited by it to the states, are reserved to the states respectively, or to the people.

Communism

Communism is a political ideology that believes societies can achieve full social equality by eliminating private property. The concept of communism began with Karl Marx and Friedrich Engels in the 1840s and then spread around the world. By the 1970s, more than one third of the world's population lived under some form of Communist rule. However, since the fall of the Berlin Wall in 1989, communism has declined but still represents the second largest form of government after democratic republicanism.

The MegaCepts of communism are best understood by studying the principles embodied in *The Communist Manifesto*, which was published by Marx and Engels in 1848. The *Manifesto* had four major parts, which become the highest level of communist MegaCepts:

- Part 1, The Bourgeoisie and Proletarians: "The history of all hitherto existing society is the history of class struggles."

- Part 2, Proletarians and Communists: "In place of the old bourgeois society and class antagonisms, we shall have an association in which the free development of each is the condition for the free development of all."

- Part 3, Socialist and Communist Literature: "There are three different types of socialist literature, or critiques of the bourgeoisie: reactionary socialism, conservative or bourgeois socialism, and critical-utopian socialism or communism."

- Part 4, Position of the Communists in relation to the various opposition parties: "The Communist Party supports all revolutionary movements that challenge the existing social and political order."

The *Manifesto* also defines ten goals of the Communist Party, which become the next level of MegaCepts:

- Abolition of property in land and application of all rents of land to public purposes.

- A heavy progressive or graduated income tax.

- Abolition of all rights of inheritance.

- Confiscation of the property of all emigrants and rebels.

- Centralization of credit in the hands of the state, by means of a national bank with State capital and an exclusive monopoly.

- Centralization of the means of communication and transport in the hands of the State.

- Extension of factories and instruments of production owned by the State: the bringing into cultivation of wastelands, and the improvement of the soil generally in accordance with a common plan.

- Equal liability of all to work. Establishment of industrial armies, especially for agriculture.

- Combination of agriculture and manufacturing industries; gradual abolition of all distinction between town and country by a more equable distribution of the populace over the country.

- Free education for all children in public schools. Abolition of children's factory labor in its present form. Combination of education with industrial production, etc.

It is interesting to think about these goals in today's world. Some, such as first and third goals, might seem "strictly communist," whereas others, such as the tenth goal, are pervasive under most governments and in most societies.

Socialism

Socialism is based on the idea of common ownership in which all the people of the world share resources and own them collectively. Under socialism, everybody would have a say in how resources are managed and utilized. Further, there would be no money, selling, or buying. All goods would be produced only for what people need. There would be free access to everything, and work would be voluntary.

Key MegaCepts groups:

- Five principles of socialism (by the Communist Party of Australia):

    - "The working class has achieved state power and exercises working class control over a completely new state apparatus—a workers' army, police, courts, and other institutions of state, including the administrative bureaucracy."

    - "There is a centrally planned economy with long-term development cycles and goals to steadily develop the productive economy to meet the needs of the people."

- "There is sectoral and representational democracy in national, regional, and local assemblies—to frame policies and to implement and monitor them."

- "There is vigorous and deep-seated participatory democracy in the workplaces and communities."

- "The role of the revolutionary party/parties is to guide and lead the masses in achieving these goals, to encourage empowerment of the masses, and to continue the revolutionary process of transforming society to liberate the full potential of all people."

- The basic principles of socialism (from Adam Buick, a leading socialist in Britain):

  - "That society, as at present constituted, is based upon the ownership of the means of living (i.e., land, factories, railways, etc.) by the capitalist or master class, and the consequent enslavement of the working class by whose labor alone wealth is produced."

  - "That in society, therefore, there is an antagonism of interests, manifesting itself as a class struggle, between those who possess but do not produce, and those who produce but do not possess."

  - "That this antagonism can be abolished only by the emancipation of the working class from the domination of the master class, by the conversion into the common property of society of the means of production and distribution, and their democratic control by the whole people."

- "That as in the order of social evolution the working class is the last class to achieve its freedom the emancipation of the working class will involve the emancipation of all mankind without distinction of race or sex."

- "That this emancipation must be the work of the working class itself."

- "That as the machinery of government, including the armed forces of the nation, exist only to conserve the monopoly of the capitalist class of the wealth taken from the workers, the working class must organize consciously and politically for the conquest of the powers of government, national and local, in order that this machinery, including these forces, may be converted from an instrument of oppression into the agent of emancipation and the overthrow of privilege, aristocratic and plutocratic."

- "That as all political parties are but the expression of class interests, and as the interest of the working class is diametrically opposed to the interests of all sections of the master class, the party seeking working class emancipation must be hostile to every other party."

Anarchy

Anarchy is the absence of government, and for that reason, not much has been theorized or written about it. According to the Oxford dictionary, anarchy is "a state of disorder due to absence or non-recognition of authority or other controlling systems."

The basic principles of anarchy (from https://dysophia.wordpress.com):

- People should be free and equal.

- People should extend aid to and be unified with each other.

Monarchy

Monarchy is a type of governing system in which a single person is the sovereign ruler of a country; the monarch has the supreme authority and acts as his/her country's head of state.

Key MegaCepts groups:

- One version of key monarchy tenets:

  - Heredity: Almost every monarchy is based on heredity, with a royal family that the monarchs all relate to.

  - Religion: Monarchies usually have a close association with their nation's religion and derive their power from it.

  - Lifelong rule: Monarchs rule for their entire lifetime, except in rare cases, and are not elected.

- Spectrum: Monarchs are all different from each other and have different amounts of power.

- The monarchy section from Saudi Arabia's constitution (general principles):

  - "The Regime in Saudi Arabia is a Monarchy. The dynasty right shall be confined to the sons of the founder, King Abdul Aziz bin Abdurrahman Al Faisal Al Saud and the sons of sons."

  - "Citizens shall pledge allegiance to the king on the basis of the Holy Qur'an and the prophet's Sunnah."

  - "The authority of the regime is derived from the Holy Qur'an and the prophet's Sunnah which rule over this and all other state laws."

  - "The system of governance in the kingdom of Saudi Arabia is based on justice, consultation 'Shoura,' and equality according to the Islamic Shari'ah (the law of Islam)."

Oligarchy

Like anarchy, oligarchy is not a specific system of government, and no country calls itself an oligarchy. Also, oligarchies can occur under any type of government, and some say that the United States is an oligarchy. Oligarchies are governments that are under the control of a few individuals or groups and usually by those who are wealthy, which is called a plutocracy and is a type of oligarchy. In democracies, oligarchs use their money and influence to manipulate the people who are elected, while in monarchies, oligarchs use their money and influence to manipulate the monarch. Sociologist Robert Michels' iron law of oligarchy holds that all organizations and societies will eventually become oligarchies, because successful people will learn how to gain more influence to their own advantage (from www.thoughtco.com).

Key MegaCepts groups:

- Eleven principles of oligarchy:

    - Reduce democracy.

    - Shape ideology.

    - Redesign the economy.

    - Shift the burden [of taxes from rich to poor].

    - Attack solidarity [make people care less about helping others].

    - Run the regulations.

    - Engineer elections.

    - Keep the "rabble" [organized labor] in line.

- Manufacture consent [materialism, market economy].

- Marginalize the population.

- Dump massive funding into militarism.

Theocracy

In a theocracy, a government or government official claims to be guided by divine forces, officials are part of the clergy of the nation's religion, and religious laws often govern society. Theocracy was more common in ancient times, but the Enlightenment forced many out of existence. In a theocracy, there is usually little freedom of expression and religion, as the government believes there is only one proper form of religion. Today, Saudi Arabia, Iran, and Vatican City are theocracies. It is difficult to combine theocracies with democracies; they are often combined with dictatorships, monarchies, and oligarchies.

Key MegaCepts groups:

- Article 2 from Iran's constitution: "The Islamic Republic is a system based on the faith in:"

  - "One God ("There is no god but God"), the exclusive attribution of sovereignty and the legislation of law to Him, and the necessity of surrender to His commands."

  - "Divine inspiration and its foundational role in the articulation of the laws."

- "Resurrection and its constructive role in explanation of laws."

- "The justice of God in creation and legislation."

- "Belief in the Imam's (*imamat*) continuous leadership, and its fundamental role in the continuity of the Islamic Revolution."

- "The wondrous and exalted status of human beings and their freedom, which must be endowed with responsibility, before God. These are achieved through:

  - "The continuous striving to reason (*ejtehād*) of qualified jurisprudents (*foqahā*) who possess the necessary qualifications based on the book (Qur'an) and the Traditions of the infallibles (*ma'sumin*), peace be upon them all.

  - "The employment of sciences, technologies, and advanced human experience with the aim of their further development.

  - "The negation of all kinds of oppression, authoritarianism, or the acceptance of domination, which secures justice, political and economic, social, and cultural independence and national unity."

Totalitarianism

A totalitarian government gives people no freedom and makes them devote their lives and ideas to the authority of the state. A strong central government forces people to follow its will. Under totalitarian rule, old political, social, and/or legal institutions are taken away and replaced with new ones to achieve the goals of the government. Under totalitarianism, people are often imprisoned and forced to perform services to the state, and violence is commonly used to reinforce authority without restraint from the law. Recent totalitarian governments include Hitler's Nazi Germany, Stalin's Soviet Union, Mao's People's Republic of China, and the Kim dynasty's North Korea.

Key MegaCepts groups:

- Yale assistant professor Christopher Lebron's article, "What Totalitarianism Looks Like," lists the signs of totalitarianism:

  - The leader insists on mass public adoration.

  - Regime controls the truth.

  - Regime suppresses knowledge producers.

  - Regime invents common enemies.

  - The leader is surrounded by cronies and sycophants.

- North Korea's Constitution (selected sections):

- First paragraph from its preamble: "The Democratic People's Republic of Korea is a socialist fatherland of Juche which embodies the idea of and guidance by the great leader Comrade Kim II Sung."

- Article 1: "The Democratic People's Republic of Korea (DPRK) is an independent socialist state representing the interests of all the Korean people."

- Article 2: "The DPRK is a revolutionary state which has inherited brilliant traditions formed during the glorious revolutionary struggle against the imperialist aggressors, in the struggle to achieve the liberation of the homeland and the freedom and well-being of the people."

- Article 19: "The DPRK relies on the socialist production relations and on the foundation of an independent national economy."

- Article 20: "In the DPRK, the means of production are owned only by the State and social cooperative organizations."

- Article 39: "Socialist culture, which is flourishing and developing in the DPRK, contributes to the improvement of the creative ability of the working people and to meeting their sound cultural and aesthetic demands."

- Article 40: "The DPRK shall, by carrying out a thorough cultural revolution, train the working people to be builders of socialism and communism equipped with a profound knowledge of nature and society and a high level of culture and technology, thus making the whole of society intellectual."

- Article 63: "In the DPRK the rights and duties of citizens are based on the collectivist principle, "One for all and all for one.""

ACKNOWLEDGMENTS

This book has been developing since my freshman year in college, so I have a wide array of people to acknowledge for their input, involvement, and support. Special thanks to:

Princeton University, where I first discovered the MegaCepts process and where my four years of education and sports taught me the discipline to think smarter and make better leadership decisions.

Our bright and outstanding director of research Brennan McDonald for his detailed and accurate research inputs.

My wonderful extended family for their encouragement and support, with special thanks to my beloved wife Roben and daughter Lara for their active involvement.

Mary, John, Neil, Todd, Ray, and Jane, who used the MegaCepts process to define the greatest thoughts on six important topics. They share their experiences and outcomes in Chapters 5 through 10.

My publishing and editorial consultants Kirsten (K.B.) Jensen , Victoria Wolf, and Patrice Rhoades-Baum.

My friends for their general encouragement and support, and particular thanks to those who took time to read my initial book drafts and provide valuable feedback.

Some fellow authors who gave me guidance on how to get my book published.

The dozens of leaders who retained me as their formal Coach to advise them on thinking smarter to make better leadership decisions.

Finally, thanks to the brilliant authors of the compelling quotations on thinking that are highlighted in this book.

ABOUT THE AUTHOR

Dave Martin, founder and managing director of 280 Capital Partners, is a Silicon Valley entrepreneur. He has been a CEO leader of four information technology (IT) companies and a strategic advisor and/or executive chairman for dozens of other IT companies. One current leadership activity of note is serving on the board of trustees of the Computer History Museum, the leading worldwide institution focused on the history of and future for all things related to information technology.

While serving in these leadership positions, Dave has coached hundreds of CEOs, executive leaders, and members of the boards of directors. His coaching focuses on how to apply more effective thinking to a company's leadership, strategic direction, and financial goals. Similarly, while serving as an officer, board member, or trustee for numerous nonprofit industry associations and educational institutions, he coaches fellow board members to apply more effective thinking to the organizations' strategic decisions.

Dave received a Bachelor of Science in Engineering degree from Princeton University, where he also started and lettered on the varsity football and baseball teams. It was as a freshman at Princeton that he first developed the MegaCepts process to arrive at your greatest thoughts on any subject; this leads to more effective thinking and decision-making in both your personal and professional life.

After graduating, he joined IBM, where he became knowledge-able in computer science and launched his career as a leader in the complex, fast-moving, and dynamic tech industry.

A Special Invitation for Readers

The author welcomes direct communication from readers!

You can reach Dave Martin by email at Dave@MegaThinkingBook.com. Plus, you can visit the Mega Thinking website (www.MegaThinkingBook.com) to share your thoughts on thinking.

For example, you can share your experience with the MegaCepts process. Did you apply this process to a topic in your personal, educational, or professional life? What was the result? Did the MegaCepts process elicit any particular insights, prompt any changes, or help you make an important decision relating to home, school, or work?

In addition, visit the website to find out about Dave Martin's latest books, articles, and lectures that further develop the power and scope of the MegaCepts process.

If you would you like to learn even more about the MegaCepts process and get guidance to actively apply it in your professional life, Dave coaches leaders at all levels. Simply contact him to inquire about a coaching relationship. In addition, he welcomes opportunities to speak to groups about his *Mega Thinking* book, including discussing the MegaCepts process and showing how it results in smarter thinking and better leadership decision-making.

Contact Dave Martin
at Dave@MegaThinkingBook.com
or www.MegaThinkingBook.com

Made in the USA
Middletown, DE
13 September 2024